BEGINNINGS

BEGINNINGS

REFLECTIONS ON THE BIBLE'S
INTRIGUING FIRSTS

MEIR SHALEV

Translated from the Hebrew
by Stuart Schoffman

 HARMONY BOOKS / *New York*

Biblical quotations that appear in *Beginnings* are based on the following
translation sources:

The Torah: The Five Books of Moses (Philadelphia: Jewish Publication Society,
1962); *The Prophets: Nevi'im* (Philadelphia: Jewish Publication Society, 1978);
The Writings: Kethubim (Philadelphia: Jewish Publication Society, 1982).
All rights reserved

The Tanach, translation copyright © D. Mandel. Found on *Davka Judaic
Classics CD*. All right reserved.

New Revised Standard Version Bible, copyright 1989, Division of
Christian Education of the National Council of the Churches of Christ in the
United States of America. Used by permission. All rights reserved.

Library of Congress Cataloging-in-Publication Data
Shalev, Meir.
[Bereshit. English.]
Beginnings : reflections on the Bible's intriguing firsts / Meir Shalev ;
translated from the Hebrew by Stuart Schoffman. —1st ed.
p. cm.
Includes bibliographical references and index.
1. Bible. O.T.—Criticism, interpretation, etc. I. Schoffman, Stuart. II. Title.
BS1158.H4S44513 2011
221.6—dc22 2010020266

ISBN 978-0-307-71718-4 (alk. paper)
eISBN 978-0-307-71719-1

Printed in the U.S.A.

BOOK DESIGN BY BARBARA STURMAN
JACKET DESIGN BY JESSIE SAYWARD BRIGHT

2 4 6 8 10 9 7 5 3 1

First Edition

Contents

Introduction

The book of Genesis, true to its name, describes the beginnings of things. Though the Bible speaks in such terms only about the creation of the world, it also portrays the first love, the first death, the first laugh, the first dream, and tells too of the people who were chosen to do things first: to give birth, to hate, to deceive; to be the first musician, king, blacksmith, or spy.

These firsts are often surprising. The first death in the Bible, for example, is not of natural causes. The first crying is not of a newborn baby or of a bereaved parent or an unrequited lover. The first dream in the Bible is not dreamt by an important figure in the history of the Jews, but rather by an utterly marginal king of the Philistines. The first kiss is not a lovers' kiss but a father's test of his son, spurred by suspicion. And the first appearance in the Bible of the Hebrew word for "love" is not about the love of a man for a woman, or a woman for a man, or a mother for her son. The first love was a father's love.

This is a book of biblical firsts, each of which gives rise to further occurrences. In writing it I kept faithful to a self-imposed rule: each of these cases has to be explicitly designated. The first love and first hatred, for example, could not be derived from an interpretation of the stories. The words "love" and "hate" had to appear in the text.

This is my second book about the Bible. The first was called *Bible Now*, and, again now as then, I neither wish nor pretend to furnish a substitute for reading the Bible itself. I urge readers to go back to the original and make new discoveries—about themselves as well.

THE FIRST LOVE

Once I happened to visit a fishing village in the Andaman Sea, west of the Malay Peninsula in the Indian Ocean. Unlike typical fishing villages, this one was not situated onshore, but floated in the sea. Its houses were built on rafts that were anchored side by side and connected with ropes and wooden walkways.

The village rocked tranquilly upon the waves, up and down, creating a strange sensation. In general, when you go from a boat to a dock, you feel at once the reassuring solidity of the shore, whereas here I went from one rocking to another.

The villagers were Muslims, Malay fishermen. I walked among their houses until I came upon a half-opened door beyond which sat a thin, wiry man. We exchanged glances and the man smiled and invited me in with a wave of his hand. We drank tea. On the wall were a photograph and a drawing. The photo was some sort of European landscape—green valleys, reddish brown cows, waterfalls, snow-covered mountains.

The drawing was readily identifiable: a young lad lying upon an altar, an old man brandishing a knife over him, an angel hovering overhead, and in the background the ram, its horns caught in the bush.

For a moment I thought I had stumbled upon one of the Ten Lost Tribes, and in my mind I began to compose letters to the Chief Rabbinate and the Jewish Agency, urging that these people be airlifted to Israel. But before throwing my arms around my long-lost brother, I asked him what was depicted in the drawing. The man pointed at the old man with the knife and pronounced, with an unfamiliar lilt: "Ibrahim." He then pointed to the lad and said: "Isma'il." I knew different, yet said nothing. When I got back to Jerusalem, I checked and discovered that indeed, according to some interpreters of the Quran, it was Ishmael and not Isaac whom God had ordered Abraham to sacrifice. I report this with a degree of embarrassment. I should have known this all along.

Instead of the requisite amazement I felt sorrow. The Israeli-Arab conflict, I realized, isn't only about land or holy places. It's a dispute over something more difficult: love. Specifically, a father's love. And to make things even more complicated, this is not love that is expressed in the gift of a coat of many colors, or by a better blessing, but rather in the very worst act to be found in the book of Genesis—the binding of Isaac. It is written in the Bible: "Take your son, your favored one, Isaac, whom you love," and offer him as a burnt offering. It's a bit hard for the heirs of Ishmael to see the name Isaac attached to the words "your favorite son, whom you love."

Ishmael and Isaac themselves, by the way, were not rivals. Certainly not like Cain and Abel, Jacob and Esau, Joseph and his brothers. The real rivalry in the family was between the two mothers, Sarah and her maidservant Hagar. The notion that two separate religions would someday spring from Ishmael and Isaac was as yet unknown. But when God said "your favored one, whom you love" about Isaac—Ishmael and his mother having been banished from Abraham's house—the emotional basis for the problem that afflicts us to this day was set in place.

But there's more: This "whom you love" is the first appearance of love in the Bible. Two points are of interest. First, that this is the love of a man for his son, not his wife. That will come second, in the love of Isaac for Rebecca. Moreover, here we have a father's love, not a mother's. The first case of motherly love will be the third instance in the Bible—the love of Rebecca for her son Jacob. Then too there is discrimination between brothers: Rebecca loves Jacob, Isaac loves Esau.

Two oddities: From a literary and societal point of view, and a legal standpoint as well, a mother's love is thought to be greater than a father's. As for love between man and wife, modern literature ranks it higher than the love of parents for their children, and indeed in the natural order of things it comes first—for without it, there'd be no children to love them in return. But the Bible favors the family, and in this case, the family that will become a nation. Thus Abraham's love for Isaac is put in first place. The love of a parent for a daughter, incidentally, is never mentioned in the Bible at all.

ADAH AND ZILLAH

Did Adam love Eve? Did Eve love Adam? Maybe so, but their relationship is not described by the word "love," which is too bad. A romantic reader would be happy to encounter the word "love" in this case in particular, for Adam and Eve were a unique couple, not merely owing to their pleasant life in the Garden of Eden, or their intimate proximity to God, but because they were the only couple in the whole world. They genuinely experienced, for quite a while, what only a few lucky couples feel on rare and fleeting occasions. Yet the Bible does not speak of any love that prevailed between the first man and the first woman. It mentions such things as shame, knowledge, labor, sadness, domination, and procreation. It informs the reader that Eve will desire Adam and he will rule over her—but it says nary a word about their love. Maybe love is unnecessary when there's no other man or woman in the world.

And so, without love, Adam "knew" Eve and Eve gave birth to Cain. Cain knew his wife—her name is unknown—and she gave birth to Enoch. Enoch begot a son named Irad, and Irad begot Mehujael, and Mehujahel begot Methusael, and Methusael begot Lamech. So it is written: begot, *yalad* in Hebrew. In general the man sires—*molid*—and the woman gives birth—*yoledet*—but here the text uses the latter verb form for men. (Maybe that's how it was, in the distant past.) In any event—there were men and women, and children were born, but love still went unmentioned.

Neither is it written that Lamech loved, but his wives, unlike the other women of those generations, did have names, and Lamech even sang them a song that he, I imagine, considered charming:

> *Adah and Zillah, hear my voice,*
> *O wives of Lamech, give ear to my speech,*
> *I have slain a man for wounding me,*
> *And a lad for bruising me.*
> *If Cain is avenged sevenfold,*
> *Then Lamech seventy-sevenfold.*

The words "sing" and "song" do not appear, but the rhythm and the Hebrew rhymes speak for themselves, and thus Lamech is the first person in the Bible to produce a bit of creative writing. Alas, this was not a love poem, but an ode to belligerence. If Lamech loved anyone, it was himself.

According to Genesis 5, Lamech was the father of Noah, he of the flood and the ark, who also had a wife. The Bible says nothing about her, though I've no doubt that she adored Noah. As usual in the Bible, here too the man is the hero of the story. Noah was a righteous man, blameless in his day; he spoke with God, built the ark. But it was Noah's wife who, while he devoted himself to his new obsession, handled the family's day-to-day affairs.

Nowhere is it written, but Noah's wife was a very loving woman, surely the most patient of all the patient women in the Bible. First she silently suffered the building of the ark, then the prolonged stay within it, a crowded and foul-smelling craft, filthy and noisy, with animals and birds inside and a raging flood outdoors, and not only hundreds of creatures but also one husband, three sons, and three daughters-in-law. No escape, no privacy—if it were up to me, I'd name the ark for her, and the whole story too. Not Noah's Ark but Noah's Wife's Ark, as she too, just like her love, is never called by name.

The Bible does not describe the hard life inside the ark. But one may gauge the situation in light of the long recovery period thereafter. When the flood was over and the earth dried off and everybody emerged from the ark, God reminded Noah and his family of the responsibility of the human species to be fruitful and multiply. Yet it took two years for a son to be born to Shem, the son of Noah. It thus turns out that in the ark everyone practiced absolute abstinence, which continued for another year!

It would appear that the crowded, claustrophobic conditions stimulated a yearning for monkish solitude, which took a good while to get over.

The son of Shem was called Arpachshad. Arpachshad begot Shelah, and Shelah begot Eber, and Eber begot Peleg, and Peleg begot Reu, and Reu begot Serug, and Serug begot Nahor, and Nahor begot Terah, and Terah begot Nahor, and Haran and Abram, the Abram who would later be renamed Abraham and be known as "Our Father," and would take for a wife Sarai, who would be renamed Sarah and give birth to his beloved son Isaac.

Sarai was a "beautiful woman," and since I am speaking of firsts, let me point out that she is the first beautiful woman in the Bible. Nevertheless, even though at last we have a man with such a beautiful wife, we are still without love. Generation upon generation has passed, and we have been fruitful and multiplied and gotten angry and killed; we have sinned and been punished; we built a city and a tower and an ark; we got drunk and cried; we banished and were banished; we laughed and made others laugh, and lied and feared; we planted vines and a tamarisk tree, and dug wells—but have still not found love. All these Hebrew verbs have appeared, but not yet this one—*alef, heh, bet,* which spells love.

And then—a surprise, a terrible surprise: "Take your son, your favored one, Isaac, whom you love, and go to the land of Moriah and offer him there as a burnt offering."

The conventional wisdom has it that the story of the binding of Isaac—the *akedah* in Hebrew—was meant to clarify that the God of Israel is opposed to human sacrifice, a commonplace ritual back in those days, as documented in Scripture. Mesha the king of Moab, for instance, sacrificed his firstborn son to his god as he faced defeat by the army of Israel. But such horrors transpired in our midst as well. Of King Ahaz of Judah it is written, "He even consigned his son to the fire, in the abhorrent fashion of the nations," and the best-known, most traumatic case is that of the daughter of Jephthah. Her father, the judge Jephthah the Gileadite, vowed that if he were victorious in battle he would sacrifice whoever was first to greet him upon his return. His daughter came out dancing with her tambourine to welcome him home, and he kept his word. The rabbis of the Talmud made sure to explain that Jephthah, had he been better versed in Torah law, could have extracted himself from his vow, but I shall not belabor the story. The reader may find it at the end of chapter 11 of the book of Judges and discover that in certain respects, the story of Jephthah and his daughter is even worse than the story of Abraham and Isaac. As for the *akedah* itself, I don't think the story is intended to combat the practice of human sacrifice, but rather to demonstrate how the obedience of the Bible's most obedient believer may lead into the darkest of alleys.

Either way, in the same verse that God orders the sacrifice of Isaac, love shows up in the Bible for the first time. It makes a dim, almost imperceptible debut due to its proximity to the horrific *akedah*, but this is no reason to ignore it. Here it is, and apart from being the love of a father for a son, it is intriguing for another reason: It appears not in the words of the narrator, nor those of Abraham. It's not Abraham who tells Isaac that he loves him, nor does the author tell the reader that Abraham loves his son, but God is the one who says it to Abraham, as if informing not only us, but also the first lover himself.

In effect, God returns here to his hallowed habit from the days of creation—assigning names. This may be helpful to all those who have wondered since time immemorial: "What is love?" In my humble opinion, it's an indulgence, since everybody knows what love is, especially when it fills the heart and also when it is absent. I would wager that Shakespeare, who coined the question "What is love?" could identify it coming and going, though even he had a hard time putting the answer into words.

Nice of God to have had this habit of giving names. Here's how he explains love to us, upon its very first appearance in the Bible. God called light "day," and darkness he called "night," dry land was "earth," and the waters "the seas," and the heavens "sky," and this, he tells Abraham, what you are feeling for your son, is called "love." And now that I have given a name to your love, take your son whom you love and sacrifice him to me as a burnt offering.

THE TWO TOGETHER

This is how the first love story in the Bible begins: "Early in the morning, Abraham saddled his ass and took with him two of his servants and his son Isaac, and split the wood for the burnt offering, and set out for the place of which God had told him."

The loving father is industrious and organized. His activity soothes him, eases his mind. He is first to appear, for he is the main character, and the only one who knows where they are going and why. Next are mentioned one donkey and two servants, and these three know nothing beyond their own tasks—to carry and to serve. After them appears Isaac, the story's supporting actor, who also doesn't know the truth, and finally the props of the play: first the firewood, mute and puzzling and intimidating; and later the firestone and the butcher knife will make their entrance. At the end God will dispatch the ram and the angel, who in his opinion will solve the whole problem, but will in fact raise other difficulties that will not, in any way, be resolved.

And Sarah? Where is she? Has she understood what's happening? Did she say good-bye to her son? Apparently not. Sarah has demonstrated in the past her ability to impose her will on Abraham, and has also proven that she is capable of casting doubt upon God's word. If she is silent, this indicates that she knows nothing. Abraham obviously made up some story, and even she, who forced him to banish his firstborn son, Ishmael, into the desert, could never imagine such a monstrous possibility as this one—the sacrifice of their son as a burnt offering.

Three days they walked together, the loving father and the beloved son, without exchanging a single word. On the third day Abraham recognized the appointed place and told the servants to wait with the donkey, and "the boy and I will go up there, we will worship and will return to you."

Here Abraham's lie is twofold. He speaks of worshipping God and not of making a burnt offering, and he promises to return in the plural "we," he and his son together. If he were to mention the sacrifice, the servants would ask now what Isaac will ask later: "Where is the sheep for the burnt offering?" If he were to say, "I will return," in the singular and not plural, the servants would realize that something is about to happen to Isaac. Who knows? Maybe this is the same thing he told Sarah: you sit here in the tent, and the boy and I will go worship God. We'll go and come back to you. Don't worry, Sarah.

"And the two of them walked together." The loving father and his son. At this point the two new participants, unrevealed in the first act, arrive onstage—the knife and the firestone, the designated implements that were hidden heretofore and now remove all doubt and confirm every fear. The loving father carried the tools: a knife to slaughter his son and fire to roast his flesh. The beloved son carried the raw materials: the wood and himself. Who knows, maybe Abraham produced the knife and flint in order to make clear to Isaac what was about to happen, and give him a chance to run for his life? Even if so, Isaac went along with him. Maybe he didn't flee because he didn't understand, or maybe he did understand and stayed anyway. But now, with the servants left behind, he dared to express what he had suspected deep inside all along.

"My father," the beloved son addressed his loving father, as if trying to confirm that the man with the knife is actually his father and not some stranger who wants to kill him. "My father"—and this is the first word they have exchanged, after three days of walking.

"Here I am, my son," answered the loving father, as if trying to confirm that their family bond is intact.

"Here are the fire and the wood, but where is the sheep for the burnt offering?"

He can't bring himself to mention the knife, but it is there too, in his father's hand.

"God will see to the sheep for the burnt offering, my son."

Thus answered Abraham, and the reader doesn't know how to parse these last words. Should the comma between "offering" and "my son" be read like a colon? Is it "God will provide the offering, my son," or "God will provide the offering: my son"? In other words, is "my son" an appellation of Isaac, or a definition of the sacrifice?

But apart from this, as readers will discern—and Abraham and Isaac too, albeit many years later—the words "my son" are the last that will ever be spoken between the two, not only in the here and now of the *akedah*, but from this moment on. They will continue to walk in silence to the appointed spot. The father will build an altar without saying a word to the son. He will tie him up without speaking, and he will wield the knife over him in the same absolute silence.

And Isaac too will not say a word or even cry out. Not as his father binds him with ropes and not when he brandishes a butcher knife over his neck. This defeatist passivity is astonishing. The text doesn't tell us how old he was; the word *na'ar*, or "lad," does not denote any specific age in biblical Hebrew. But it is clear that Isaac was not a small, weak child. He traveled on foot for three days and then climbed to the mountaintop with firewood on his back. For his part, Abraham was already well past his hundredth birthday.

According to the rabbis of the Talmud, Isaac at the time was thirty-seven years old. If he had wanted to, he could have run away from his father or fought him and easily saved his own life. But it appears that from the moment he realized what was happening, he was struck dumb with terror, and perhaps it was something deeper: that not just Abraham was on trial, his son Isaac was too. In any case, this story has not only protagonists but an author, who like other biblical authors has a purpose in mind, and from the outset this author has assigned Isaac only one role, that of sacrifice in the theater of the *akedah*.

Moreover, the author carries to an extreme the usual method of biblical writers, who describe actions in detail but thoughts and feelings minimally. It has often been observed that the thoughts of Abraham and Isaac are not described here at all, and their talk is doled out in snippets.

I said earlier that the words "my son" would be the last ever to be uttered between the two. But this is not just for fear of confrontation, or because the father and son stopped speaking to each other, but because from that time on they simply never saw each other again. The Bible never states this outright, but it's possible to derive it from the text. When Isaac and Abraham took leave of the two servants, it is written: "And the two of them walked together." But after the *akedah* it says: "Abraham then returned to his servants." And where is Isaac? And what happened to "together"? From now on, the word "together" will apply to Abraham's walking off with the servants: "And they departed together for Beersheba." From this we may conclude that Isaac did not return with his father, but left the place alone.

In the ensuing chapters it becomes clear that from the day of the *akedah* until Abraham's death, a period of many years, the two are not to be found "together" even once. It's possible to understand Isaac. After experiencing a father who hides the truth from you, ties you up on an altar, and waves a big knife over your neck, you might not want any more of that "together-ness." From this point on, Isaac avoided his father until the latter's death, at which time he buried him together with Ishmael, whom the same father had cast out into the desert. It is not made clear to the reader whether they came to pay their last respects or to make sure he was dead and buried.

Here one should note that the *akedah* drove a wedge not merely between father and son. We will no longer find Sarah at Abraham's side either. After the *akedah*, Abraham settled immediately in Beersheba, whereas she, at the start of the next chapter, perhaps upon hearing the news about her son, died in Kiryat Arba. The Bible tells us: "Abraham came to mourn for Sarah and to bewail her." If so, it means he has not been with her. He came from Beersheba to Hebron, to bury her in the Cave of Machpelah.

In any event, the *akedah* and the resultant fissures in the family also have a broader (if less theatrical) significance, for they illustrate what may well befall other families similar to Abraham's: the families of revolutionaries, military commanders, great scholars, and other leaders, who are devoted with all their heart and might to a vision, an idea, to art, society, science, to radical reform. In this regard, the binding of Isaac is not just a theological parable but an example of what can happen to close family members of such notables. They are forced to pay the price for ideals that were imposed upon them, revolutions they did not choose.

But the *akedah* led to another disconnection too—between Abraham and his God. Earlier, the two spoke and met quite often. God told Abraham to "go forth" from Haran, promised him the Land on several occasions, revealed himself to him in the "Covenant Between the Pieces" of Genesis 15, changed his name, and demanded that he circumcise himself; God had lunch at Abraham's tent, where for a second time he promised that a son called Isaac would be born to him, discussed with him the number of righteous men in Sodom, told him to obey Sarah and banish Ishmael and Hagar, and ordered him to sacrifice Isaac as a burnt offering.

All this came to an end. From the *akedah* onward there is no further mention of meetings or conversations between Abraham and his God. Abraham passed the test, but it would seem that the two now prefer not to see each other anymore, as though the *akedah* was a breaking point for both of them. God did not reveal himself or his word to Abraham again, nor did Abraham turn to him and seek his presence. The death of his wife and estrangement of his son showed him what a high price his family had been forced to pay. And who knows, perhaps God too had second thoughts. Maybe he repented for what he had done, or maybe he was no longer interested in this sort of faith or believer.

AND HE TOOK HER AS HIS WIFE AND
HE LOVED HER

Time passed, but did not, as is commonly hoped and supposed, heal all wounds or lessen the pain. The mother has
died, and the beloved son is forty years old and still alone, without a wife. The father knows how this came about, and also
knows he won't be able to talk to his son about it, or anything
else, from the *akedah* onward.

Talking is impossible, but taking action is not. Abraham,
whose relationships with his sons ended up with the expulsion
of the first and the binding of the second, decided to do something more. Until now, in compliance with God's will and intent, he was the father of a people, of a multitude, "our father
Abraham." Now, on his own initiative, he will be the father of
Isaac alone. The damage has been done, but Abraham will be
able to repair it, just a little.

At last, after long years of obedient acquiescence, Abraham
did something of personal significance without getting instructions from his God or his wife. In contrast with the two horrors
he perpetrated at their command, banishing Ishmael and binding Isaac, this deed was a good deed: Abraham sent his servant to Haran, to find and bring a wife for his son. A wife who
will make his life easier, comfort him, fill his heart with love.
The rift between the father and the son was so deep and absolute that Abraham couldn't send Isaac himself there, the way
Rebecca would send Jacob in the next generation. He couldn't
even tell him about it. The servant went on his mission unbe-
knownst to Isaac.

And so a small caravan arrived in Haran, Abraham's home-town in Mesopotamia: a few men, headed by Abraham's servant, and ten camels, laden with provisions and valuable gifts. The servant parked the caravan near the well outside the city, let his weary camels kneel and rest, and asked God for a sign. He suggested to the Almighty that he would ask the maidens who draw water from the well for a drink. The one who replies, "Drink, and I will also water your camels," would be the one that God has intended for the son of the servant's master Abraham.

It should be noted that this servant was not necessarily Abraham's majordomo Eliezer, as is commonly held, but there is no doubt that he was a smart and serious person. The sign the servant thought up was not just any sign, but one that served both his immediate needs and his greater goal. A maiden who would say, "Drink, and I will also water your camels," would make a good wife for Isaac—generous, resourceful, strong, kind, self-confident. And indeed Rebecca the daughter of Bethuel, granddaughter of Abraham's brother Nahor, came to the well with her jug on her shoulder. The servant asked her for water. She said: "Drink, my lord," and gave him some, adding: "I will also draw water for your camels, until they finish drinking." Her words were not identical to those stipulated by the servant, but the words were less important than the readiness and good character that stood behind them.

Again and again she drew from the well and emptied the jug into the trough, until all the camels had drunk. This entailed a lot of heavy lifting. Ten camels drink a great deal of water after a long journey. Abraham's servant was thrilled. He gave her a nose ring and bracelets made of gold, and she hurried home to tell her family about him. Her brother, Laban by name, the same Laban who will later cheat Jacob, was very excited by the sight of the expensive gifts. He ran to the well and invited the visitor to his home, along with his camels and men.

The twenty-fourth chapter of Genesis is one of the most detailed narrative passages in the Bible. The most interesting thing about the writing is the way the author repeats the events—once in the third person, describing the journey of the servant to Haran and the encounter with Rebecca and her family, and again in the first person, as the servant tells the family the same story.

I won't go into all the details, many of which are related with relish by the skilled and seasoned author, but it should be emphasized that the sign that the servant designated was indeed significant. Rebecca was revealed as a young lady who was not only generous and virtuous, but also independent and decisive. Her family members were well aware of this, and when the servant declared his wish to leave right away and take her with him, they replied in words seldom heard in the Bible: "Let us call the girl and ask for her reply."

"They called Rebecca and said to her: 'Will you go with this man?' And she said: 'I will go.' "

She and her maidservants mounted the camels and rode after the servant, who brought her straightaway to Isaac, who then dwelt in the Negev desert, near Be'er Lahai-Roi.

"Isaac went out walking in the field toward evening," as the author describes the scene. Isaac, it will be recalled, is forty and still a bachelor, a situation that even today arouses the attention of readers, friends, and family, and all the more so in the days of the Bible. His evening stroll testifies to his loneliness and solitude, to free personal time, fixed habits, comforting routines. All this will suddenly be undone by the appearance of Rebecca, and the Bible's description of their first meeting is so beautiful that I will quote it in full:

> *And Isaac went out walking in the field toward evening*
> *And, looking up, he saw camels approaching.*
> *Raising her eyes, Rebecca saw Isaac.*
> *She fell from her camel and said to the servant,*
> *"Who is that man walking in the field toward us?"*
> *And the servant said, "That is my master."*
> *So she took her veil and covered herself.*
> *The servant told Isaac all the things that he had done.*
> *Isaac then brought her into the tent of his mother Sarah,*
> *And he took Rebecca as his wife. Isaac loved her,*
> *And found comfort after his mother's death.*

"He loved her" in biblical Hebrew is expressed in a single word: *vaye'ehaveha*, an elegant condensation of feeling, time, man, and woman. Here we finally arrive at the first love of a man for a woman in the Bible. Isaac's love for Rebecca.

IT IS NOT THE PRACTICE IN OUR PLACE

The signature line of that first encounter is very touching: "Isaac was comforted after his mother's death." The verse describes, only after Sarah is gone, the deep bond that had existed between mother and son. It also shows that things are never simple and one-sided in any family. In the view of many readers—including me, I must admit—Sarah is often seen as a bad woman, and now and then as a real witch. She abused Hagar and forced Abraham to banish her and Ishmael. Yet she was a good and loving mother to Isaac. It could be that her insistence on banishing Ishmael, which in Abraham's opinion and that of many readers was an evil demand, was perceived by Isaac as a good move by his mother on his behalf. She, as opposed to Abraham, would not have obeyed God's command to sacrifice Isaac as a burnt offering, and the *akedah* doubtless proved to Isaac that he could trust and love only her. Her death was another big blow after the trial on Mount Moriah.

"Isaac then brought her into the tent of his mother Sarah, and he took Rebecca as his wife. Isaac loved her, and found comfort after his mother's death." It turns out, then, that Isaac had preserved the tent of his dead mother, and we may assume that her possessions and household goods were still in it. He thus created a portable memorial for his mother, which traveled with him wherever he wandered. One can imagine him sitting in it alone at times, to commune with her memory, maybe even living there to maintain a feeling of her enduring presence.

Bringing Rebecca into the tent is a symbolic presentation to his mother of his wife-to-be, even if the former is dead, and a request for her approval. But there is something more: Isaac is saying to Rebecca that his mother, whom she alas has never known, remains an important figure in his life even though she is gone. He is telling her too that he expects that she will take his mother's place.

Along with the story of Rebecca and Isaac comes a general statement of biblical principles regarding love. The order of Isaac's actions—bringing Rebecca into Sarah's tent, taking her as his wife, and loving her—is the proper sequence, per this point of view. Isaac was given a woman chosen by God and identified by God's sign, he took her to his mother's tent, he married her, and only then did he fall in love with her.

This brings to mind the totally different sequence of events in the case of Jacob and Rachel, in the next generation: Jacob met Rachel at the well, he kissed her even before introducing himself as a kinsman, and loved her even before she became his wife; seven years of unfulfilled love passed until their wedding day, and so enormous was his longing that he rudely said to her father: "Give me my wife, for my time is fulfilled, that I may consort with her." This disruption of protocol did not go unnoticed. God enabled Laban to trick Jacob and give him Leah in Rachel's stead.

It is usually remarked, and rightly so, that Jacob was punished because he had previously tricked his father Isaac. Indeed, it's easy to see the resemblance between the two incidents. Jacob pretended to be his brother, and Leah pretended to be her sister. Jacob did so at his mother's initiative; Leah at her father's. And the two deceptions occurred under cover of darkness—the blindness of Isaac, the night of the wedding. But Jacob's comeuppance was twofold. Not just the forced marriage to Leah, whom he didn't love, but also her fertility as opposed to Rachel's barrenness: "The Lord saw that Leah was hated and he opened her womb; but Rachel was barren."

All this was intended to clarify for Jacob the proper sequence of events and the priorities of the Bible: In first place come family and procreation, and love only afterward. For us contemporary readers, egocentric romantics for whom the happiness of the individual is paramount, this seems awful. But by the standards of those days—so things must be.

The morning that Jacob awoke and opened his eyes and saw, "there was Leah," shocks the reader to this day. It's easy to understand his anger and humiliation, and maybe even to identify with the hatred he later felt for Leah. But the Bible, through the voice of Laban, seeks to explain to Jacob that there are official rules, even in love.

"It is not the practice in our place," he made clear to Jacob, "to marry off the younger before the older." But directed at Jacob, the words "it is not the practice" point to other principles, beyond the marital customs of Haran. Here again is an expression of the biblical view of love: the womb trumps the heart. The family comes before the married couple. This is why "multiply and bear fruit" is the first command issued by God to man, and why a parent's love is the first one in the Bible, and only later comes the love of a man for a woman.

The Israeli poet Yehuda Amichai stressed another important point in this story—that Rachel and Leah, who in the Bible are two discrete personalities representing two ways of life, are likely to be bound up together in every woman. He wrote:

Every woman making love is Rachel and Leah trading off
body and soul between them, seasons and dresses, kohl
    and perfumes,
the tastes of day flavored with the spices of night,
night stirrings with day sounds, thighs and breasts, to
    become one body,
Rachel and Leah, Racheleah. It's as if Jacob were in bed
    with two women,
one stormy and fiery, knowing she will die soon in
    childbirth,
the other placid and soft and heavy, down the generations
till me.*

*From "The Language of Love and Tea with Roasted Almonds," in Open Closed Open: Poems by Yehuda Amichai, transl. Chana Bloch and Chana Kronfeld (Harcourt: New York, 2000).

And indeed reading further in the biblical story, especially later on when the unloved Leah gives birth and the beloved Rachel is barren, the thought arises that not merely in the story at hand, featuring the two sisters, does the man discover in the morning that "there was Leah." From the Bible's point of view, every man, on every wedding night, goes to bed with Rachel, the beloved for whom he lusted for seven years, and wakes up the morning after with Leah, whose role it is to bear children and raise a family. Not romantic. Not pleasant. But such is love, according to the Bible.

I do not mean to be pejorative. In the biblical view, this metamorphosis is necessary. As I said before, the Bible, especially the book of Genesis, does not glorify the love that initiates a relationship, but rather the love that develops between two people after the wedding and grows together with the family. In this regard one may recall the grim fate of two other biblical couples whose relationships commenced with love: Amnon's love for Tamar, which led to rape and hatred on his part; and Samson's for Delilah, which brought his ruin and death.

Writes the author of Ecclesiastes: "Enjoy happiness with a woman you love." But Ecclesiastes is an uncharacteristic voice from a variety of standpoints, not the biblical norm. God instructed Adam and Noah to multiply and bear children, not to work on their relationships, and he promised Abraham many descendants, not a loving life with Sarah. The same lesson may be derived from Rebecca's love for her son Jacob. She deceived the husband who loved her, for the benefit of her beloved boy.

The Bible tells us: "Isaac loved Esau because he had a taste for game; but Rebecca loves Jacob." This account indicates several things. First, that the Bible is more frank and honest than its readers. It admits the possibility that the love of parents for their children may be similar in intensity but not identical in nature. Second, that Isaac's love for Esau was conditional. He loved Esau because he provided him with tasty meat. But Rebecca favored Jacob with a love dependent on nothing at all, certainly not upon good food.

Moreover, the verse uses different verb forms for Isaac and Rebecca. Of him it is written *vaye'ehav*, suggesting a discrete event in a narrative, like "he went" or "he said" or "he ate." But Rebecca's love for Jacob is related in the present tense— *ohevet*—reflecting a permanent, ongoing condition, as if speaking about the way of the world. The sun rises in the morning, the moon is full or new, rivers run to the sea, and Rebecca loves Jacob. And indeed, in time of need, this love of the mother for her favored son will grow stronger than her love for her husband or her other son.

As for Esau—it may be that his father's preference for him is connected with the old grudge that Isaac bore against his own father, and is a way of expressing it. Isaac promoted the son who differed in appearance and occupation from Abraham, and from himself: the hairy, red-complexioned son, an anomaly in the family of the patriarchs, a hunter in the fields, a vocation reminiscent of Esau's uncle Ishmael. In addition, one should not underestimate the aromatic allure of freshly killed game, perfectly cooked.

Anyone who expected the *akedah* to turn Isaac into a vegetarian was mistaken. According to Genesis 27, the scent of meat influenced him powerfully, owing in part to his fondness for Esau's cooking, and perhaps also because the blindness that afflicted him in old age had sharpened his other senses. There's no doubt that it wasn't just Rebecca's scheming, but also Isaac's gluttony, that tipped the scale on that fateful day against the son he loved more. Despite his suspicions, and despite Jacob's clearly identifiable voice, Isaac's lust for the food addled his brain, permitting Rebecca and Jacob to trick him and damage Esau.

The episode recalls what happened two chapters earlier, when Esau sold his birthright to Jacob for a bowl of lentil soup. It thus becomes clear that Isaac handed down to Esau an unbridled passion for food and an inability to delay gratification, whereas Rebecca gave Jacob a talent for scheming and deceit. Maybe this too is a reason that Rebecca loved Jacob and Isaac loved Esau. Each loved the son who resembled him or her.

AND ABRAHAM TOOK ANOTHER WIFE

Let us return to Abraham. Even now, after his plan had been realized, and Isaac married Rebecca and was consoled over his mother's death, the father and son did not live together. The split between them had not healed. One may assume that Isaac knew that Abraham had orchestrated his marriage to Rebecca. The slave had told him "all the things that he had done," and obviously servants do not pick up and travel to far-off lands and bring women from there for the sons of their masters on their own initiative. Still, the connection between Isaac and his father was not restored.

To Abraham's credit it may be said that he chose a good and proper way to help his son. He had also obviously hoped to draw him closer. But even if Abraham was disappointed, he didn't express it. He also did the right thing by not insisting that Isaac pay him back with a renewal of relations or expressions of gratitude. It was enough to know that he had benefited him, and the reader soon realizes that he benefited himself as well.

Indeed, immediately after Isaac took Rebecca for a wife and loved her, Abraham took himself a wife as well, a much younger woman named Keturah. And even as his son and daughter-in-law waited twenty years for their first pregnancy, the old man speedily sired many sons by his new wife.

Do not take this lightly. When he was a hundred years old, Abraham doubted his ability to beget Isaac. Now, at the age of more than a hundred and forty, and minus the visitations of angels and tidings or promises from God, he fathered six sons by Keturah, one after the next: "She bore him Zimran, Jokshan, Medan, Midian, Ishbak, and Shuah."

The old father's marriage, so closely following that of his son, and his astonishing fertility, so much greater than the latter's, and the cute rhyming names of the little boys that trip merrily off the reader's tongue, represent a joyful flowering. Indeed, there is little doubt that Abraham has changed for the better. The *akedah* distanced him from his son but released him from the demanding omnipresence of his God and his wife, the two figures who ran his life with a heavy hand and made him commit such dreadful deeds as banishing his firstborn son and offering the other as a sacrifice.

Now, with God silent and Sarah dead, and Isaac comforted by his love for Rebecca, Abraham finally found time for himself. He became a highly active and productive senior citizen. Apart from Keturah, he had concubines who also bore him children. The Bible emphasizes, of course, that Isaac was and remained the favorite son, to whom Abraham bequeathed all that he owned, and that Abraham sent away the sons of the concubines to the land of the East, lest they compete with the son of Sarah. But this is not what's important. The big story is Abraham's metamorphosis at such a ripe old age. He finally shed his role of father of a nation and a faith, quit being a symbol, and turned into a private person. Again he undergoes a great transformation, which is more personal and happier and lovelier than the national and religious metamorphoses that preceded it, than the trek from country to country, the change of name and the circumcision.

Indeed, not only Abraham but also his traumatized organ ceased serving as a symbol, and returned to its normal, pleasant function. It was no longer obligated to fly the flag of the covenant and supply the seed for the whole Jewish people. Now it becomes simply the happy flourishing organ of a man freed from his demanding God and difficult wife. And instead of a tied-up son and a deported one, who would fight from time immemorial until this very day over his love, Abraham sires ordinary kids, and instead of being the "father of a multitude of nations" he is the husband of many concubines and father of a flock of children.

Abraham dies in ripe old age. "Old and contented," as the Bible has it, and the reader senses that at last he is satisfied, relaxed, even blissful. Ishmael, the son he expelled from his home on his wife's orders, and Isaac, the son he bound on the altar at his Lord's command, buried him together. I said earlier that maybe they showed up to make sure he was dead, but now it seems clear to me that Abraham's fine old age has a healthy effect on the reader too, and on the way he or she understands the story. Now I sense the forgiveness for the father on the part of the sons, maybe even remorse that they hadn't reconnected with him while he was alive.

The two buried Abraham alongside Sarah, nemesis of one of

them and mother of the other, in the Cave of Machpelah, which many centuries later would also become a locus of discord. But it's doubtful that Abraham knew this, and even if he did, it's doubtful he would have cared. He lived well during his last good years, with his new wife and concubines and children. Now, after his death, he again finds himself alongside Sarah, who barely recognizes him, so good does he look.

THE FIRST DREAM

When you hear "dream," and especially "the first dream," you tend to think immediately of the dream of the ladder and the angels that the patriarch Jacob dreamed at Bethel, and about his son Joseph, whose entire path was paved with dreams. Unfortunately, the Bible's first dreamer was not one of our forefathers but rather a certain Philistine, whose name was Abimelech, king of Gerar. The subject of Abimelech's dream—and I am not sure this will please or console the reader—was our mother Sarah, wife of Abraham.

Our mother Sarah, as I have already reported, was a very beautiful woman, and our father Abraham had the strange and perverse habit of introducing her as his sister and handing her over to foreign kings for their sexual pleasure, lest they harm him because of her. He first did this with the pharaoh in Egypt, then with Abimelech in Gerar. By the way, according to the book of Genesis, Sarah was ninety at the time, but maybe Abimelech preferred mature women, or else was himself two hundred years old, an age not uncommon among the main players in Genesis, and liked to rob the cradle. Either way, Abimelech took her unto him, and that very night dreamed the first dream in the Bible.

"You are to die because of the woman you have taken," said God to him in his dream, "for she is a married woman."

So far as I know, this is the first time the expression "to die for" appears in the Hebrew language, but here its meaning is different from its usage today. Not "crazy about" or "blown away by" or some other romantic hyperbole, but dead because of her, plain and simple, punished for the sin of taking a married woman.

Indeed the Philistine king is terrified. "Will You slay even righteous people?" he asked God, and pleaded innocent: "He himself said to me, 'She is my sister!' And she also said, 'He is my brother.' When I did this, my heart was blameless and my hands were clean."

Abimelech returned Sarah to her legal husband and was spared punishment, and one more thing should be noted— there had been no consummation, as my grandmother used to say about such situations. In other words, Abimelech didn't get around to enacting his designs upon Sarah, which was a good thing, since the next chapter opens with the announcement of her pregnancy. That's all we need, for Isaac to be rumored to be the bastard son of some uncircumcised Philistine, aspersions to be cast upon his status as son of our father Abraham, not to mention the implications for the Middle East of today.

To return to our subject, it so happened that this Abimelech, and not such luminaries as Abraham, Isaac, Jacob, or Joseph, gets credit for the Bible's first dream. Notwithstanding the angst that this might cause a Jewish reader, there is a solid and simple definition here of the purpose of dreams: the voicing of divine news. Not all biblical dreams were as clear and straightforward, nor did God appear in them all. Yet the dream in the Bible is not a complicated psychological vehicle, but rather a simple, practical tool by whose means God has his say. Just as two generations later Joseph—"that dreamer," in his brothers' mocking words—will say of the dream of the king of Egypt: "God has told Pharaoh what He is about to do."

HE LAY DOWN IN THAT PLACE AND HAD A DREAM

The first dream of the Hebrews was the one I mentioned above, the dream of Jacob in Bethel in Genesis 28. During his flight from the angry Esau, on his first night away from his mother's tent, far from her supportive proximity, Jacob slept in a field. "Taking one of the stones of the place, he put it under his head and lay down in that place. He had a dream; a ladder was set on the ground and its top reached to the sky, and angels of God were going up and down on it."

The description "its top reached to the sky" recalls the words "its top in the sky," used earlier in Genesis to describe the Tower of Babel. As elsewhere, the biblical author created a similarity between the two stories for the purpose of showing the differences between them:

The Tower of Babel was built in reality; the ladder appeared in a dream.

The Tower of Babel was built before the human race had been divided into nations; whereas the ladder is a Jewish project.

The Tower of Babel was erected by many well-organized people, unified in thought and speaking a single language, the dream of Jacob is a unique dream of one individual.

The Tower of Babel was a declaration of war against God, but Jacob's ladder symbolizes a connection with God.

But the dream amounted to more than just a ladder and angels. God appeared in it too and stood beside Jacob. Since this was their first meeting, he began by introducing himself: "I am the Lord, the God of your father Abraham and the God of Isaac," and then repeated the promise he had made to them too: "the ground on which you are lying I will give to you and to your offspring."

The content of the promise is similar, but its wording offers a lovely and moving innovation. In promising the land to Abraham, God said: "Raise your eyes and look out from where you are, to the north and south, to the east and west, for I give all the land that you see to you and your offspring forever." By contrast, God defined the land he promised Jacob in the dream as "the ground on which you are lying." The seeing eye takes in a wider landscape than the lying body, but seeing lacks the intimate contact with the ground. Thus the bond between Abraham and the land is the cool and fleeting look of the eye, a distant and abstract connection, typical of the sense of sight. But Jacob has full and close contact with the land, one body touching another, man and earth, *Adam* and *adama*.

Some readers may be troubled, I suspect, by the small dimensions of "the ground on which you are lying." Let me calm them with the news that the rabbis of antiquity were also bothered by the problem, which they solved in a satisfying fashion. On that night, they explained, God folded up the whole Land of Israel under Jacob's body, and the next morning unfolded it and spread it out anew. The explanation is nice, but it misses the real significance of the situation as described in the text.

The issue here is not the boundaries of the land, because in any case one can't define them either by eye or by lying down. What this is about is the quality of the connection with the land. This is a land with which Jacob will have a physical connection, a loving bond.

Two other promises of the land come to mind, which greatly resemble one another. One is the promise God made to Joshua son of Nun, on the eve of his entering the Land of Israel: "Every spot on which your foot treads I give to you." The other is the vow Moses made to Caleb son of Jephunneh: "The land on which your foot trod shall be a portion for you." Let me note parenthetically that not only are these two promises alike, but so are the two heroes who received them. Joshua and Caleb were the two spies who were not afraid of the inhabitants of the land, and advocated taking it by force. Forty years later, Joshua led the nation in conquering and settling the land, and Caleb himself conquered his tribe's portion.

And so, unlike the farseeing eyes of Abraham and the marching feet of Joshua and Caleb, unlike God's promises of sweeping vistas or crushing conquests, God's promise of the land to Jacob is a promise of contact, of full sensual connection, between a man and his land. To put it more broadly, the God who promised the land to Abraham and Joshua is the God of the first chapter of Genesis, who abstractly spoke his world and its creatures into existence, and commanded man to conquer it and control them. But the God of Jacob's dream is the God of Genesis 2, who created man from earth—*adama*—with his own hands, and gave him its name, *Adam*.

IF GOD REMAINS WITH ME

Now God returned and sounded the familiar refrain of "Your descendants shall be as the dust of the earth," and pledged to Jacob that a vast nation would spring from his loins. Considering his prior speeches to Abraham and Isaac, it's reasonable to assume that if it were up to him, the dream would end here. But Jacob luckily remembered that this was his dream, and so God was compelled to turn from the grand national destiny of the Jewish People in the distant future to the immediate and distressing personal problem of the dreamer—his long and frightening journey from his mother's tent in Canaan to his kinfolk in faraway Haran.

"I am with you," God reassured him. "I will protect you wherever you go and bring you back to this land. I will not leave you until I have done what I have promised you."

The words are surprising and moving. Even Abraham didn't get a personal assurance like this on the eve of his journey in the opposite direction. And let's not forget that Abraham set out on his way by divine command, whereas Jacob's journey was his mother's idea.

Jacob woke up. "Surely the Lord is present in this place," he said, "and I did not know it." He was fearful—"How awesome is this place!"—and he realized: "This is none other than the abode of God, and that is the gateway to heaven." He lay there till morning, maybe fell back asleep, and when he got up he poured oil on the stone he had used as a pillow and changed the name of the place from "Luz" to "Bethel," which means "House of God."

Then Jacob made a vow, a vow much more important than God's words in the dream, because God hadn't said anything basically new or deviated from what he had said in the past, whereas Jacob's vow redefined the relationship between God and man. Out of the faith and awe, the joy and trembling, that permeated the dream and his awakening, burst his voice, a new bold voice the likes of which not only the reader, but also God, had not heard before.

"If God remains with me," he said, "if He protects me on this journey that I am making, and gives me bread to eat, and clothing to wear, and if I return safe to my father's house, the Lord shall be my God."

At first glance, this is just a listing of technical details connected with the trip, but let us not be mistaken. Jacob's very first word—"if"—announces to God that here is a new type of believer. First of all, the word casts respectful doubt, suggesting the possibility that God's promise might not be fulfilled. Second, since "if" is conditional, it offers a deal: If the Lord keeps his word, he will be Jacob's God. And if he doesn't? The answer is unspoken, but it hangs in the air, clear and logical: he will not be my God. Maybe he will be someone else's, but he won't be mine. I'll find myself some other gods.

The impression made by Jacob's words was so powerful that five hundred years later, when the Torah was handed down on Mount Sinai, God began the Ten Commandments thus: "I the Lord am your God who brought you out of the land of Egypt, the house of bondage," and only then continued, "You shall have no other gods beside me." In other words, he first established that he had met the conditions, kept his promise, and only then demanded that he be the sole God of Israel. He had remembered and taken to heart the conversation with Jacob, the ancient patriarch of the Children of Israel who now stood at the foot of the mountain. He spoke to them this way so that they would not be able to tell him "if," so that they would not set conditions as their ancestor Jacob had done.

BREAD TO EAT, AND CLOTHING TO WEAR

But Jacob didn't leave it at that. He also took the language of the offer God made him in the dream, examined it closely, and like a good lawyer handed it back with comments and corrections. The reader will appreciate his meticulous intelligence.

First let us return to God's original offer to Jacob: "I am with you. I will protect you wherever you go and bring you back to this land. I will not leave you until I have done what I have promised you."

And now Jacob's response to God: "If God remains with me, if He protects me on this journey that I am making, and gives me bread to eat, and clothing to wear, and if I return safe to my father's house, the Lord shall be my God."

The differences are Jacob's emendations, and they are interesting and instructive.

God offered: "I will protect you wherever you go."

Jacob's improved version: "If He protects me on this journey that I am making."

That is, I'm not interested in general promises; I want protection on this specific trip, from here to Haran and back.

God said only "I will protect you," to which Jacob added the clause: "And gives me bread to eat, and clothing to wear." In other words, it is not enough just to ensure my survival; God also has to provide a standard of living and quality of life.

God promised: "I will bring you back to this land."

Jacob's correction: "If I return safe to my father's house."

He added the word "safe"—*b'shalom* in the Hebrew—to make plain that he would not be content simply with returning but was insisting on coming back in good shape. And just as he had earlier specified "this journey," he altered the broad wording "back to this land" to "my father's house." Meaning that he wanted more than to return anyplace inside the borders of the country; he wanted to come back to the family he had been compelled to leave. In essence, he is saying that his father's house, his family, is more important to him than the land God has just promised him.

There's more: "To this land" might also be interpreted as a return to the same place he is at the moment. But since Jacob has just named the place "Bethel," House of God, he may mean this: I don't want to return to your house, I want to return to my house.

God's offer, and Jacob's improvements thereon, indicate the conflict of interests between them. God has a master plan and sees the big picture. Abraham, Isaac, and Jacob are merely stepping-stones on the path he has designed, no more than rungs on his ladder. But in contrast to Abraham, Jacob was unwilling to take on this job as offered. He made clear to God something that should have been made clear to God long before: that not only God, but also the specific person standing before him, has demands that must be taken into consideration. Even if that person is chosen for an important national and historic role, he has personal needs in the here and now, pressing problems of his own. "Wherever you go" reflects God's encompassing field of vision. "This journey that I am making" is the specific reality Jacob must deal with now, including such minutiae as clothing and food, which don't concern God at all.

And more important still: As I said, the opening "if" sets a clear condition before God and establishes that if he didn't fill it, he would have to find himself another believer. Underlying this condition is the concept that God needs Jacob just as Jacob needs God. And from now on, God knows that Jacob knows this too.

This is also the meaning of the angels that Jacob saw in his dream. They go up and down the ladder and thus become a symbol of a symmetrical, two-way connection. They travel between Jacob and God in both directions and represent the give-and-take of both sides. True, the top of the ladder is up and the bottom down, but the movement of the angels establishes a kind of equality between the two.

To God's credit it should be noted that though he may have been surprised, he did not react harshly to Jacob's brazen words. So far as I can tell, after the initial shock there was even a rush of affection on God's part. Until now, he had believers who were foolish and childish, like Adam and Eve, resentful and murderous like Cain, righteous and obedient like Noah and Abraham, insolent like the builders of the Tower of Babel, wicked sinners like the generation of the flood and the residents of Sodom—and suddenly comes this skeptical and demanding believer, a different mental type entirely, almost impudent, but so bold and original and interesting.

Meanwhile, Jacob has added another line: "And this stone, which I have set up as a pillar, shall be God's abode." Meaning, in this place I will build a sanctuary.

It could be that the author put these words in Jacob's mouth because he himself lived in a later period, a time of well-established organized religion, and needed to deliver an opinion about the income of the priestly caste. But I hope that he wanted to give Jacob another bold wink at the heavens. When he promises God he will build him a house, Jacob again points to the similarity between them. The difference between us is not that great, he tells him; we both have material needs. And just as we've taken care of my clothing and food, let's also guarantee your house and sacrifices.

And, indeed, in the very next verse he says: "And of all that You give me, I will set aside a tithe for You." This too is a condition: If I get from you, I'll give to your priests. Since a tithe means ten percent, Jacob makes clear to God: the amount I give to the priests depends on how much you give me. One can sense the smile on his lips, as if to say: Let's not be disingenuous. Let's not hide behind that fanning out "to the west and to the east," and those descendants as numerous "as sands on the seashore," and the other lofty language and grandiose promises. We both know that religion is not just faith and prophecy, not just a promised land and chosen people and prophetic ethical diatribes. It's also a sanctuary, priests and altars, sacrifices and tithes. It's Chief Rabbis, religious deal makers and politicians and *kashruth* inspectors, and they all have to make a living.

Let me say parenthetically that Jacob's calculation of tithes also reflects something else, regarding his areas of personal interest. The first words Jacob uttered in the Bible, at the end of Genesis 25, were "First sell me your birthright," directed to Esau. His last words, at the end of Genesis 49, spoken on his deathbed to his sons, were "The field and the cave in it, bought from the Hittites." Jacob in his lifetime knew love and desire, bereavement and longing, loss and pain, fear and the overcoming of fear. But the Bible preferred to emphasize the business side of his life, beginning with a sale and ending with a purchase. And so, as a maker of deals and contracts—not as a righteous fool or obedient yes-man, but as he stood facing Esau and will stand facing Laban and the figure he will wrestle at the Jabbok crossing—Jacob, in his dream, also stands up to God.

FAR BE IT FROM YOU

J acob was not the only believer to bargain with God, nor the
first. Before him came Abraham, who in Genesis 18 argued
and bargained with him over the number of righteous people for
whose sake Sodom would be spared. There is an apparent similarity here between the two patriarchs, grandfather and grand-
son, but what really draws our attention is the difference between
them, as reflected in the difference between the two conversations.

It will be recalled that "three men" paid a visit to Abraham to deliver the news that his son Isaac would be born to
him. Two of the guests were the angels who went from there to
Sodom, in order to destroy it. The third was God, who stayed
with Abraham for another brief discussion. It began in a promising and surprising fashion. Abraham asked God boldly, almost
insolently: "Will you sweep away the innocent along with the
guilty? What if there should be fifty innocent within the city,
will You then wipe out the place and not forgive it for the sake
of the innocent fifty who are in it? Far be it from you to do such
a thing, to bring death upon the innocent as well as the guilty,
so that innocent and guilty fare alike. Far be it from you! Shall
not the Judge of all the earth deal justly?"

The length of Abraham's speech, its rhythm and tone, tes-
tify to his great agitation. This was not his first meeting with
God, but usually God spoke and Abraham listened. Now Abraham had a unique opportunity. God was a guest in his tent and
ate lunch with him, and he could engage God in a real conversation. His main motive, in my opinion, was his concern for the
fate of his nephew Lot, who lived in Sodom. But this is plainly
also an essential discussion of reward and punishment, even an
opportunity to criticize God's decision and try to change it.

Abraham's emotions, however, caused him to confuse various notions and claims. His opening argument was "Will you sweep away the innocent along with the guilty?" which resembles the question of Abimelech, king of Gerar: "Will You slay even righteous people?" In other words, he did not object to the slaying of the wicked of Sodom, but was concerned only for the innocent residents. But then he had a new idea: Would God forgive the whole city on account of fifty righteous people who might be there? Then he set that aside, and went back to the first argument: "Far be it from You to do such a thing, to bring death upon the innocent as well as the guilty."

"If I find within the city of Sodom fifty innocent ones, I will forgive the whole place for their sake," said God. In other words, he chose to ignore the subject of collective punishment, and preferred to spar with Abraham not on a matter of principle but instead about the number of innocent people for whose sake the city would be spared.

Abraham fell into the trap. He started to bargain with God like a haggler in the market: "Here I venture to speak to my Lord, I who am but dust and ashes. What if the fifty innocent should lack five? Will you destroy the whole city for want of the five?"

"I will not destroy it if I find forty-five there," said God.

"What if forty should be found there?" said Abraham.

"I will not do it, for the sake of the forty," said God.

"Let not my Lord be angry if I go on," Abraham said, pressing his luck. "What if thirty should be found there?" One can almost hear him adding, "I can't afford a penny more."

But God displayed patience even now: "I will not do it if I find thirty there."

"I venture again to speak to my Lord," said Abraham. "What if twenty should be found there?"

"I will not destroy it for the sake of the twenty," said God, wondering if Abraham will ever get to the heart of the matter.

"Let my Lord not be angry if I speak but this last time," asked Abraham again. "What if ten should be found there?"

"I will not destroy it for the sake of the ten," said God, and got up and left. As it is written: " 'I will not destroy, for the sake of the ten.' When the Lord had finished speaking to Abraham, He departed."

God shows his impatience. He is saying: Get to the point. You've taken up too much of my time haggling over trivia. But his leaving is also an act of disappointment. God expected that Abraham would speak the truth, that he was worried over the fate of Lot, and would not hide behind a theological discussion. But even if he was interested in a theological conversation Abraham should have conducted it properly and taken advantage of the rare opportunity for a genuine investigation of ideas.

Two issues are embodied within Abraham's bargaining with God: One is collective punishment, punishing the righteous together with the wicked, which Abraham broached but didn't pursue. The second is the value of the righteous individual, which Abraham tried to address, but with the stratagem of a merchant.

God's impatient departure may be taken to mean that there is no difference between forty righteous men or twenty, thirty or ten. Yet there is a difference between many righteous people and one. Hence the enduring Hebrew expression: "One righteous man in Sodom," a good person among scoundrels. But Abraham didn't go into that subject, and when God saw that Abraham was trying to lower the price without clarifying the truly important issue, he was fed up: "When the Lord had finished speaking to Abraham, He departed."

By the way, Abraham's questions had been answered in the past. Had he read the story of the flood, several chapters and generations before him, he would have realized that God saves the one righteous man, but does not forgive the evil ones for his sake. Back then, he saved Noah, the one righteous man of his day, and wiped out all the sinners. So will God do now too in Sodom: His angels will save the one righteous man, namely Lot, and destroy the whole town and all its sinful inhabitants. In short, this whole standoff was superfluous from the outset, and Abraham missed a chance to have a serious discussion with his God.

Now, back to Jacob. From a first reading of the dream of the ladder, it would seem that Jacob, unlike his grandfather, didn't even attempt a discussion of principles, but preferred to bargain over technical details and his personal needs for the journey to Haran. But despite the fact that Jacob dealt merely with his needs of the moment and Abraham, ostensibly, with larger ethical questions—it turns out that Jacob was the deeper and more thoughtful of the two. Not only did he establish that the relationship between God and man is two-way and symmetrical, that God needs his believers just as they need him, but he went further still. He made it clear to God that man needs him to protect him on his journey and provide him food and clothing, whereas God depends on his believers for his very existence.

Thus God came to understand that decrees such as "Go forth from your native land" and tests of faith such as the *akedah*, which worked fine with the obedient Abraham, would be unacceptable to Jacob. God would test him too, but differently. Jacob would not be called upon to perform one hideous deed, but rather to endure ongoing trials. The first of these would be the journey to Haran, a challenge Jacob would meet handily. He started out scared and worried, and finished strong and bold, as evidenced by his rolling the heavy stone from the mouth of the well and kissing Rachel at their very first meeting. The second test would be the long wait for his beloved, and here too he would succeed. The third trial would be her prolonged barrenness, which Jacob would not handle well, but along the way he would learn a lesson about himself and his love. The fourth trial would be the false bereavement he was made to suffer, when he believed that his son Joseph was dead. Not only had his other sons lied to him and concealed the truth from him, even God had not appeared to him in a dream or otherwise revealed to him that Joseph was still alive.

But Jacob withstood yet another test, as described in Genesis 32. This was the nocturnal struggle at the ford of the Jabbok River, one of the most cryptic and fascinating episodes in all the stories of the patriarchs.

WHAT IS YOUR NAME?

On the eve of his encounter with Esau, twenty years after he had fled from his brother's wrath, Jacob again requested assistance from his God. Previously he had been a lad who left his mother's tent, frightened and empty-handed—"with my staff alone I crossed this Jordan," he recalled twenty years thereafter—and now he returned as the head of a large family, accompanied by a great many livestock.

But in both instances his heart is filled with dread. Back then, because of the hardships and perils of the road, and now, because of the impending meeting with his brother. Then, he asked that God attach a safe return home to the deal they made, of which he now reminds him: "Deliver me, I pray, from the hand of Esau; else, I fear, he may come and strike me down,

expressing his confidence in the God of Israel: "You come to me with sword and spear and javelin; but I come to you in the name of the Lord of hosts, the God of the armies of Israel, whom you have defied." This declaration was intended not only for the ears of the adversary, but was directed mainly toward the Israelites, the ones who heard him then and the ones who read his words today. David was telling them, and the rest of us, that their new leader, and not some ordinary shepherd, was fighting their battle.

Each one of his words is carefully chosen. He asked for God's help, but made sure to address his enemy in the first person singular. "This very day the Lord will deliver you into my hands. I will kill you and cut off your head; and I will give the dead bodies of the Philistine army this very day to the birds of the air and to the wild animals of the earth," and only then did he again mention God: "All the earth shall know that there is a God in Israel."

This is not just a warrior psyching himself up. It is the continuation of the course David took from the moment he arrived at the battlefield, a vector of leadership. It could be that he is talking this way because he had been anointed king by Samuel in the previous chapter, but the victory over Goliath and the anointment are actually two separate stories, as I have already suggested and will soon endeavor to prove.

And as the fuming Philistine drew closer, David ran toward him, raising Goliath's hopes of face-to-face battle, but once within range David took a stone from the pocket of his robe, whirled the sling, shot the stone, and hit Goliath in the forehead: "The stone sank into his forehead, and he fell facedown on the ground. Thus David prevailed over the Philistine with sling and stone, he struck the Philistine down and killed him; there was no sword in David's hand. Then David ran and stood over the Philistine; he grasped his sword, drew it out of its sheath, and finished him off; then he cut off his head. When the Philistines saw that their champion was dead, they fled."

The fact that David drew Goliath's sword from its sheath tells us that Goliath had not yet taken it in hand. From this the reader may deduce the great distance from which David slung the stone, so far away that Goliath saw no need to draw his sword. But it also demonstrates the literary method of the storyteller, which encourages the reader to infer one thing from another, and does not spell everything out.

His writing talent is apparent in another narrative nuance. Consider the second sentence I've just quoted: "Thus David prevailed over the Philistine with sling and stone; he struck the Philistine down and killed him; there was no sword in David's hand." In Hebrew, this sentence, in style and meter, sounds like a line from a song, different from the prose narrative that surrounds it. It might be part of a song that was sung in those days about the battle of David and Goliath, perhaps a line alongside "Saul has slain his thousands, David his tens of thousands," which appears soon in the biblical text. I would even speculate that this very line testifies that such a battle actually did take place. For if the author had invented it, he would have invented an entire victory song, like the song in the book of Exodus that follows the splitting of the Red Sea; he would not have incorporated a line from an existing song into his story.

Let me note, parenthetically, something similar in the story of the concubine and the Benjaminites of Gibeah, which we discussed previously. Amid the dry description of that battle, we find one line that in Hebrew seems plucked from a victory poem, now lost, commemorating the event. The King James Version renders it nicely: "Thus they inclosed the Benjaminites round about, and chased them, and trode them down with ease over against Gibeah toward the sunrising." Then the biblical writer reverts to his normal prose: "And there fell of Benjamin eighteen thousand men."

As for the story at hand: from time immemorial, generations of schoolchildren have learned about the battle of David and Goliath, always in the same way—the little guy defeated the giant. The weak bested the strong. The servant of God trounced the idol worshipper. But in my opinion, it is worthwhile reading the story another way: the smart one beat the dummy. The one with originality defeated the conservative. Improvisation beat preconception, invention trumped routine.

Here lies the true significance of the words Saul spoke to David: "You cannot go against this Philistine and fight him, for you are just a boy, and he has been a warrior from his youth." Saul meant that "a warrior from his youth" was an advantage and "just a boy" was a deficiency, but the results proved that the opposite was true. Goliath had been a warrior from his youth, a battle-tested veteran, and ongoing military experience, for all its advantages, is also a source of conservatism. David won by virtue of new thinking, by ignoring the stodgy conventions of hand-to-hand combat, by using inventive and unexpected weaponry—and, of course, with the help of God.

WHOSE SON ARE YOU, MY BOY?

I noted earlier that the Bible offers the reader two versions of David's ascent to the throne. One version has him anointed in secret, brought to Saul as a musician, and made his trusted servant. According to the other story, David was a young shepherd who came to visit his brothers on the battlefield and killed

Goliath. The biblical editor attempted to work a verse into the Goliath story to connect the two versions and make them into one. When he described how Jesse sent David to his brothers, the editor added an awkward explanation: "David went back and forth from Saul to feed his father's sheep at Bethlehem." In other words, he is indeed Saul's musician and arms-bearer, but from time to time goes home to help his father graze the sheep, and from there he was sent to visit his brothers on the field of battle.

It's an interesting attempt, but it doesn't work. First of all, in time of war the king's arms-bearer is supposed to be with his master at the scene of battle. It makes no sense that he would go graze his father's sheep in the desert, especially since only three of his brothers had gone to fight the Philistines, leaving four more brothers at home who could have tended the sheep. What's more important is that according to the account of the Goliath story, Saul didn't know David at all. He even asked his military commander, Abner son of Ner: "Whose son is that boy, Abner?" And Abner answered: "By your life, Your Majesty, I do not know." How can it be that the king didn't recognize the person who plays music for him and carries his weapons? How can it be that the military commander didn't know who David was?

The same words recur after the victory. Abner son of Ner brought David, Goliath's head in hand, before Saul. The king asked: "Whose son are you, my boy?" And David replied: "The son of your servant Jesse the Bethlehemite."

I read these spare and ordinary words and am filled with emotion and envy. What a talented author this is, able to instill a tone of curiosity and suspicion in Saul's question, and of confidence and threat in David's answer. His words are so simple: "The son of your servant Jesse the Bethlehemite." But their tone says that Saul had better remember this name, and not forget it.

All of the foregoing supports the assumption that the music story and the battle story are two separate stories, despite the editor's attempt to combine them. If the David who killed Goliath was the same one who played music for the king, Saul would have surely said: "I thought you were just a musician . . ." But Saul didn't know David at all. He took a look at this ruddy and handsome lad, and at the giant head of Goliath in his hand, and understood that not only had Goliath been vanquished this day, he had been too.

Indeed, two men were struck down on that day in the Valley of Elah. Goliath lost his head, and Saul lost his crown. Neither of them imagined the extraordinary qualities of the young man who stood before them, but in Saul's case there is an added irony, for it should have been he who went out to face Goliath with a shepherd's sling in his hand. First of all, he was the only Israelite endowed with great height—he may even have been as tall as Goliath—and, more important, Saul was from the tribe of Benjamin, who were famously accurate slingers. We have already read in the Gibeah episode, which serves as background to the whole saga of Saul, about the warriors of Benjamin: "Every one of them could sling a stone at a hair and not miss."

It's even possible to assume that Saul's proficiency with a sling was greater than David's, but Saul, like Goliath, was "a warrior from his youth," a man of preconceived principles by which one does not go into one-on-one combat with sling and stone, but with armor, javelin, helmet, and sword. First you throw the javelin—as in the combat depicted in Homer's *Iliad*— and then, if necessary, you come closer and continue face-to-face with swords. Those are the rules followed by Saul and Goliath, and they lost. David decided to play by his own rules, and he beat them both.

AND SAUL WAS DAVID'S ENEMY

N ow begins a new phase in Saul's life and reign. If until now he was forced to deal with the zealous and uncompromising Samuel, now he also had to struggle with the charismatic and talented young David. In one sense, this latter struggle is easier, since David is not a man of God. Talented as he may be, he is a man like Saul, not a prophet who can work wonders and see the future. On the other hand, the struggle with David is more complicated, because Saul's relationship with Samuel was based on fear alone, whereas his relationship with David included love, hate, awe, and jealousy, which together made an impossible mix of emotions.

When they met in the first story, when David was brought to play music for Saul, the king loved him very much and made him his arms-bearer. But in the second story, after David's victory over Goliath, the feeling that flooded Saul was completely different. When the women sang, "Saul has slain his thousands, David his tens of thousands," jealousy, that most destructive and enduring of emotions, welled up within him, followed by hostility: "And Saul regarded David with hostility from that day and onward." Indeed, from then on, David became the main issue in Saul's life. All the king's energies, his entire agenda, were devoted to a single goal: to get rid of his rival.

The first attempt occurred right after the victory over Goliath. An evil spirit came over Saul, "and he prophesied in the midst of the house." The verb "to prophesy" in this particular grammatical construction is used in the Hebrew Bible to connote religious ecstasy, loss of control, excitement, and madness.

Saul had had a tendency toward such prophesying even beforehand. Right after he was anointed, he joined a group of prophets and prophesied with them, arousing considerable perplexity among those who knew him. Their perplexity was so great, in fact, that their reaction—"Is Saul also among the prophets?"—became a figure of Hebrew speech from that day onward. Saul repeated this behavior after David—with the aid of his wife Michal, Saul's daughter—escaped from the assassins the king had dispatched to his home. Saul then stripped off his clothes and prophesied naked in front of Samuel. Such a tendency to prophesy bespeaks a complex and intriguing personality, if exercised in moderation, but it proves yet again that this man was not fit to be king of Israel.

To return to the present instance: "An evil spirit from God gripped Saul, and he prophesied within his house, while David was playing the lyre, as he did daily. Saul had his spear in his hand; and Saul threw the spear, for he thought, 'I will pin David to the wall.' But David eluded him twice."

The author, and perhaps the editor, again tries to unite the Goliath story with the music story, this time in a much smoother and more effective fashion, but the critical element is Saul's failed attempt at assassination. David managed to dodge the flying spear, the king tried a second time, and David again got away. I remind the reader that this was at close range, inside a room, on the part of a big-boned and practiced warrior. The double miss tells us that David was quick, alert, and agile, but it mainly testifies to Saul's mental state at that moment. Indeed Saul interpreted his failure the same way: "Saul was afraid of David, because the Lord was with him and had departed from Saul."

Fear, as the reader well knows, was not a new feeling for

the king. He was already afraid of the people, and of Samuel, and now he is also afraid of David. But this fear is combined not only with jealousy and hostility, but also with love, which was the first feeling he had for David, in their first story together.

"And he loved him greatly," is how their asymmetrical relationship began, and that love carried on. Love works like that. If David had done Saul a great wrong, betrayed him, cheated him, stolen from him—that love might have lessened, but even then, it would likely have not disappeared. But David had not hurt Saul that way. He hurt him through his charm, his talents, his nobility of mind, his capacity to win the love of others, including Saul himself. He hurt him because things came so easily for him. He hurt him by his very existence, his essence. In effect, everything that had aroused love for David in Saul's heart would from now on arouse hostility, jealousy, and fear. He loved him, feared him, and wanted to kill him.

Saul could no longer bear to have David around him. Perhaps he was afraid that he would again do something terrible if David came before him again. He decided to keep him away from the royal court and appointed him captain of a thousand soldiers. This was not a logical move for a king, a ruler who bestows authority and promotes his subordinates; it was a great mistake, a blunder driven by emotion. The appointment to a senior military position removed from the court enabled David to operate without close supervision and to build his own power base, far from the king's gaze and control. Indeed David succeeded greatly in his new job, "and he went out and came in before the people." To "go out and come in," in biblical language, means to lead, and Saul's fear of him only grew. "He dreaded him," says the text. In the emotional gradient of Hebrew, dread is stronger than fear.

Now Saul tried to get rid of David in a different way, craftier and more complicated. He offered him Merab, his elder daughter, for a wife, but in exchange demanded that he go fight the Philistines. "Let not my hand be upon him, but let the hand of the Philistines be upon him," said Saul, hoping David would fall in battle. But Merab married someone else, so Saul offered David Michal, his second daughter, who he knew loved David.

David became suspicious: "Does it seem to you a small matter to become the king's son-in-law, when I am but a poor man, and insignificant?" In other words, I have no money for a bride-price worthy of a princess. Saul leapt at the opportunity and said he would ask for no money, and be content with one hundred Philistine foreskins. On hearing this request, the reader is permitted a smile. So far as we know, only Jewish males who are eight days old are prepared to surrender their foreskins without objection. Mature gentiles are likely to fight like tigers against anyone seeking to relieve them of this tiny treasure. Saul hoped that David would be killed in his attempt to gather the required bride-price, but David continued his string of victories, returning to the royal palace with no fewer than two hundred foreskins.

What great distress this bright-eyed young redhead caused Saul, appearing first as a virtuoso lyre player, next dangling the severed head of a defeated giant, and another time bearing bushels of Philistine foreskins. It was clear to Saul that only divine assistance could have brought such success. "Saul grew still more afraid of David; and Saul was David's enemy ever after."

DO I LACK MADMEN?

The next attempts to do away with David were more blatant, and so was Saul's agenda. He discussed the need to kill

David with his slaves and with his son Jonathan, but Jonathan revealed the plot to David and managed to convince his father to give up his murderous plans. Saul even swore to his son, "As the Lord lives, he shall not be put to death," and David returned to the palace. But when David scored another victory against the Philistines, the evil spirit again overtook his hunter.

This time, as I reported earlier, Saul sent assassins to David's house, but the plot was thwarted by the king's daughter Michal. She chose to be loyal to her husband and not her father, warned him of the killers lying in wait, and let him escape undetected out the window.

Chapter 20 of the First Book of Samuel marks the high point of Saul's hatred for David. The reader can study it and learn the details. I recommend paying close attention to Jonathan's devotion to David. Jonathan, who was a bold and famous warrior, much beloved by the people, already knew that David, and not he, would inherit the throne of his father Saul. He loved David "as he loved his own soul," and asked only that David swear never to harm his future descendants.

Saul, with ample justification, interpreted Jonathan's affinity for David as a betrayal of him and his family. At a new peak of insanity he again let fly his spear, this time not at David but at Jonathan, his own flesh and blood. This time too he missed, and the reader understands that this series of misses reflects not only bad aim and confusion, but also Saul's reluctance to do actual damage as he desperately strained to express the depth of his despair.

As for David, from this point on he did not return to the palace. He went to Nob, the city of priests, pretending to be on a secret royal mission, and there stocked up on food and arms. Not just any arms—he took the sword of Goliath, which had been stashed there for safekeeping. From there he continued onward to the worst of his enemies, the Philistines, and not just any Philistines, but into the lion's den itself, to Achish the king of Gath, hometown of Goliath.

Going there with the sword of Goliath in his hand shows incredible boldness, and also created a serious problem. The servants of Achish identified him at once, so David feigned madness, drooling into his beard and scratching marks on the doors of the city gate. Achish grew angry with his servants, and in his rage uttered one of the finest lines in all the Bible: "Look, you see the man is mad; why then have you brought him to me? Do I lack madmen, that you have brought this fellow to play the madman in my presence?" It appears that Philistines had a sense of humor—superbly rendered, incidentally, by the Zionist firebrand Ze'ev Jabotinsky in his novel *Samson*—humor with which the Israelites of the period were not endowed, or if they were, the authors of the Bible took pains to censor it.

From there, David fled to the Cave of Adullam, and Saul continued to pursue him. The king's mental state deteriorated further. In a fit of paranoia he accused all of his intimates, first and foremost his son Jonathan, of treason. He did not rest content with throwing spears or dispatching assassins. He brought in the army, and began by massacring all the inhabitants of Nob. Nob was the town of the priests who had aided David, and Saul's warriors smote "both men and women, children and babies, and oxen, and asses, and sheep." The wording drives home the author's message: Saul did to the priests of God what he had refused to do to the Amalekites.

Then Saul went hunting for David in the Judean desert and the south Hebron hills, leading an army of three thousand soldiers. The number three thousand is not incidental. When Saul established his monarchy, he created an army of exactly this size. It is thus made clear to the reader that all the king's soldiers were now engaged in chasing after David.

And, indeed, from this point till the end of his life, apart from one more war against the Philistines, Saul spent his time on nothing else. "And Saul sought him every day, but God delivered him not to his hand," we read in First Samuel 23. Yet they did have one touching encounter, evidence that Saul's feelings for David remained complex. David and his men, roughly four hundred in number, were hiding in the depths of a large cave, when Saul entered "to cover his feet," as the Hebrew has it—presumably to wash them, and rest in the pleasant coolness, and perhaps relieve himself. David's men urged him to seize the moment and kill the man who sought to slay him, and David slipped around behind the king, but did no more than cut off the corner of his cloak.

"God forbid I should do this thing to my master, the Lord's anointed, to stretch forth my hand against him, seeing he is the anointed of the Lord," David said to his men. There's a sarcastic tone to his remark, but I prefer to interpret it as a statement of principle. David is making clear to his men that a King of Israel, any King of Israel, is the Lord's anointed, and it is forbidden to harm him under any circumstances. From this the reader understands that while the first king was obsessed with pursuit, at the expense of his royal duties, the second king was laying the foundations of his future monarchy.

As Saul walked away from the cave, David came after him and called out. Saul turned around and David showed him the piece of cloth he had secretly cut from the king's cloak. He said he could have killed him but did not. "I have not sinned against you, yet you are bent on taking my life," David said. "May the

Lord judge between me and you! May the Lord avenge me on you; but my hand shall never touch you."

He even called Saul *"Avi,"* "my father," and when Saul heard his words he burst into tears. "Is this your voice, my son David?" he sobbed, and the reader senses the real root of the matter. For all his hostility and his fear of David, and despite the many talents of his brave son Jonathan, David is the heir he wished for. And perhaps, from the moment Saul realized that David would in fact succeed him, he needed to call him his son. The love he felt for David had not waned, and he knew David was in the right, but his tears tell us that his mental problems were too much for him. He told David he knew he would reign after him, and made him swear never to harm his descendants. David swore, but unlike his similar promise to Jonathan, this one he would not fulfill.

MAY YOU BE BLESSED, MY SON DAVID

Saul also did not keep his promise. His tormented soul got the better of him, and again he went after David, in the Wilderness of Ziph. Again David had an opportunity to kill him, when he found the king and his bodyguards asleep, and again David said to his men: "The Lord forbid that I should lay a hand on the Lord's anointed." This time, David took the spear and water jar of the sleeping king.

The two stories—the cloth-cutting in the cave, and the spear, jar and sleeping guards—are very similar, and neither makes much sense. It seems impossible that four hundred soldiers could be hiding undetected in a cave, and highly unlikely that the king would walk in there unescorted and without prior surveillance. Nor would three thousand men all fall asleep together, leaving their king unguarded. Even the Bible comments that this was a sort of miracle—"a deep sleep from the Lord had fallen upon them"—and it might be that these are tall tales, fanciful war stories such as soldiers have spun from time immemorial.

In any case, David climbed to a hilltop and from there called out to Abner son of Ner, the commander of Saul's army, and taunted him for not keeping proper watch over his king. "And Saul knew David's voice, and said, 'Is this your voice, my son David?'"

The language is the same as in the cave story, and again Saul promised to stop pursuing David. Once again he said this in front of all his soldiers, indicating another mental breakdown of a man steered only by his emotions, and not by logic or wisdom. David, for his part, was unimpressed. He already knew his adversary well, and that he could not rely on his promises. Not because the king was a liar or scoundrel, but because he was mentally ill.

Saul took his leave with the words, "May you be blessed, my son David. You shall achieve, and you shall prevail," and went home. But David was not reassured. Again he sought refuge with Achish the king of Gath, but this time he did not show up alone or need to impersonate a madman. He arrived at the head of his battalion, a force not to be taken lightly. Achish was duly impressed, and gave David the town of Ziklag as a home base.

In those days, the Philistines were organizing for another war against Israel. They gathered their army at Shunem, north of today's city of Afula. The depth of their penetration into the land of Israel shows how Saul's grip on the north of the country had weakened while he and his army had been busy running after David in the south. At the beginning of Saul's reign, Israel was in such sorry shape that the Philistines had a standing army at Geba, in the territory of Saul's own tribe, and the Israelite army had to assemble farther east, in the Jordan Valley. But by the time David killed Goliath, the field of battle had shifted westward, to the Valley of Elah, adjacent to Philistine territory. In other words, Saul had managed to push the enemy back toward their own cities by the sea and in the coastal plain, but now, when he was preoccupied with the incessant pursuit of David, the Philistines grew stronger and had reached the eastern part of the Jezreel Valley.

On the eve of battle Saul was filled with dread. God had not answered him. Not in his dreams or through God's worldly representatives. In his distress he asked his servants to find him a medium, a woman who could raise the spirits of the dead. Saul had previously commanded that wizards and mediums be purged from the land, but it turned out that one such woman remained in Endor, not far from his military camp at Mount Gilboa. Saul put on plain clothes and went to her. I figure that he walked along the *wadi* or riverbed that runs between today's Kibbutz Geva and Kfar Yehezkel, to avoid detection by Philistine lookout posts, and cut through the low-lying area at the foot of the hill of Moreh.

This walk is very symbolic, because the medium is a portal into the depths of the grave and the depths of the mind and soul. This was Saul's final submission, his embrace of the darkest roots of his spirit. Going to the medium was the start of his journey to death.

The medium did not recognize the king. She even said to him: "Behold, you know what Saul has done, how he has expelled those who are mediums, and the wizards, from the land; why then do you lay a trap for me, to get me killed?" But the moment she raised the ghost of Samuel for him, she realized who Saul was. She shrieked: "Why have you deceived me? You are Saul!" But the king calmed her down, and asked her what she saw. "And she said, 'An old man comes up, and he is wrapped in a robe.' Then Saul knew that it was Samuel."

I see Samuel's robe as his trademark garment, akin to Elijah's mantle. Samuel's custom of always wearing a robe originated in his early childhood, when his mother Hannah gave him over to the House of the Lord at Shiloh. The "little robe"—these are the Bible's touching words—was the gift she would bring on her annual visit to her son who grew bigger each year, and it became the symbol of her love, and her main connection with him. I imagine that Samuel's enormous rage after the war with Amalek, when Saul clutched and accidentally tore the hem of his robe, derived from Samuel's deep emotional bond with this garment.

Samuel's words to Saul at the house of the medium serve as proof that for all the lofty encomiums customarily declaimed at funerals and memorial services, death does not improve the dead. The dead Samuel is like the living Samuel. Even after his death he has not lost his beloved robe and his nasty personality. He was and remains the same grudge-bearing, vengeful man of faith, a cruel fanatic. Now, he reminded Saul of his great sin of yore, when he took pity on the king of the Amalekites and also failed to slaughter all their livestock, and informed Saul that the next day he and his sons would die in battle.

Predictably, Samuel's words put Saul in a panic. He had not eaten a thing all day, and now he collapsed. The medium feared for him and prepared him a meal to revive him, and Saul agreed to eat only after she and his servants insisted. He returned to his camp with clear knowledge of what was to come, and acceptance of his fate.

Knowing he would die, Saul embarked on his final campaign. And it was in this very battle, the one that claimed his life, that he proved that within his tormented soul lurked great power. He could have fled, surrendered, or retreated to regroup. But he went to war knowing he would lose his life, and his suicide begins here, before he fell on his sword.

The Philistines won a big victory and the Israelite army fled on the heights of Gilboa. Anyone familiar with the local terrain knows that the northwest slopes of the mountain are especially steep and bare. Philistine soldiers killed Saul's sons, and their archers spotted him and began shooting their arrows. Saul was especially afraid of arrows. He asked his arms-bearer to slay him with his sword so that his enemy could not make sport of him. The arms-bearer refused, and each fell on his own sword and died.

The next day, when the Philistines came "to strip the slain," to gather weapons and loot the belongings of the dead, they found the bodies of the king and his sons. They cut off Saul's head and sent it to their country together with his weapons, to display them as trophies of victory. His beheaded corpse and the bodies of his sons they fastened to the wall of Beth-Shean.

"When the inhabitants of Jabesh-Gilead heard what the Philistines had done to Saul, all their valiant men set out, and walked all night long, and took the body of Saul and the bodies of his sons from the wall of Beth-Shean, and came to Jabesh and burned them there. Then they took their bones and buried them under the tamarisk tree in Jabesh, and fasted for seven days."

DAVID GREW STRONGER AND STRONGER

Someone standing today on the eastern peaks of the Gilboa range, on Mount Malkishua or Mount Avinadav, named for the fallen sons of Saul, can see the nocturnal route of the men of Jabesh-Gilead. To the southeast, Wadi Yabes—a dry creek mentioned in the Bible—runs from the Gilead to the Jordan. The men walked westward, turned north in the Jordan Valley, and reached Beth-Shean. They removed the bodies of Saul and his sons from the city wall and returned the same way they had come. All this in one night of courage and supreme effort—a final act of gratitude to the man who had saved their fathers and their city at the beginning of his reign, many years before.

This was the last journey of King Saul, but from the same spot one can also see the route of his first military campaign, against the Ammonites. Saul went along the Bezek stream south of the Gilboa, eastward to the Jordan River, split his forces in three, attacked the Ammonites, and saved Jabesh-Gilead, the city whose males had been put to death and maidens kidnapped several generations earlier, in order to secure the perpetuity of his tribe, the tribe of Benjamin.

It would seem that we might end here, on a note of setting things right, of satisfaction and closure. Peering from the peaks of Gilboa at the routes of Saul's last and first campaigns, we could say that a story that began with the gruesome tale of the Levite and his concubine, leading to a bloody civil war and the leveling of a city and abduction of its maidens, worked out in the end with tribal loyalty, succor in time of need, and a final gesture of respect for the fallen. But the story wasn't yet over. Saul and his sons were dead, but people from his family remained alive, and their fate is of significance.

Immediately after Saul and sons died on the Gilboa, David went from the desert to Hebron, and there declared himself king of Judah. He well knew who remained from the house of

Saul. First among these was Abner son of Ner, Saul's military commander and uncle. It is not clear what Abner did or didn't do in the war at Gilboa, why he was spared or how he escaped, but clearly he did not die there. Now he was the strong man in Saul's family and royal court, and the one man likely to endanger David. Also remaining were Ish-Bosheth son of Saul, Mephibosheth son of Jonathan, and Rizpah daughter of Aiah, the concubine of Saul, and her sons by him. Saul had given his daughter Michal, who had previously been David's wife, to one Paltiel son of Laish, and she and her sister Merab had possibly borne grandchildren to Saul. It is worth examining what happened to these people, and to the whole house of Saul.

The first thing David did as king was to express appreciation to the men of Jabesh-Gilead for the kindness they had shown Saul after his death, and promised to reward them. "Therefore now let your hands be strengthened, and be brave," concluded his message to them, "for your master Saul is dead, and also the house of Judah have anointed me king over them."

Here David showed considerable political savvy. The men of Jabesh-Gilead were the staunchest of Saul's loyalists and had demonstrated their devotion, competence, and fortitude. He spoke warmly to them, also making clear the new balance of power. Interestingly, David at this time did not approach Abner son of Ner, as if to declare that he considered him unimportant. Abner, for his part, crowned Saul's son Ish-Bosheth as king of Israel, and the clash between the two political entities, southern and northern—it's hard to call them kingdoms or states—soon followed.

The place: the pool of Gibeon, in the territory of the tribe of Benjamin, near the border between Judah and Israel. The participants: Abner son of Ner and his men from the house of Saul;

and on David's side, his kinsmen Joab, Abishai, and Asahel, the sons of Zeruiah, and their men.

Abner suggested: "Let the young men come forward and sport before us."

"Yes, let them," said Joab.

From this sport developed a real battle. Three hundred soldiers of Israel died, and twenty men of Judah. It was obvious who had won, but one of the casualties of Judah was Asahel, brother of Joab and Abishai, and his killer was Abner son of Ner. Readers expecting revenge will not be disappointed.

"There was a long war between the house of Saul and the house of David," says the Bible. "David grew stronger and stronger, while the house of Saul became weaker and weaker." David established himself, took wives and sired children, while the house of Saul was caught up in rearguard battles and internecine feuds. Abner son of Ner slept with Rizpah the daughter of Aiah, Saul's former concubine. Saul's son Ish-Bosheth rebuked him for it, and Abner got very angry. He informed the frightened Ish-Bosheth that he intended to hand over the kingdom of Israel to David, who would rule from Dan in the north to Beersheba in the south, and he did just that. He sent messengers to David, offered him a pact, and promised to persuade all the tribes of Israel to come under to his rule.

David agreed on one condition: that his first wife, Saul's daughter Michal, who had been given to Paltiel son of Laish, be returned to him. This was not the demand of a loving husband who missed his wife, but of a king with a political agenda. The Bible does not describe the couple's happy reunion, but rather Michal's parting from her second husband and his prodigious weeping, upon which I shall elaborate later.

After his demand was met, David invited Abner to Hebron

and threw a banquet for him. The two worked out their next moves and Abner headed home. At the same time, Joab and his soldiers returned to Hebron. Joab heard about Abner's visit, and the news that his brother's killer had been hosted by David incensed him greatly. One may assume that Joab was also insulted by having been kept in the dark, and perhaps he even feared that Abner would be given the post of military commander as part of the deal. He presented himself before the king, claimed that Abner was plotting espionage, and without telling David he sent men to bring Abner on a phony pretext back to Hebron, where he slew him at the city gate.

David knew how to make the best of a bad situation. He ordered up a grand funeral for Abner and led an orchestrated display of grief and sorrow, including weeping and fasting. It was important for him to show that he had nothing to do with Abner's murder, though everyone knew at the time that Abner's death was very useful to him, as does anyone who reads the story today. It may be found in Second Samuel, at the end of chapter 3.

As for Ish-Bosheth son of Saul, the puppet-king of Israel, he was killed by two brothers, military captains, who cut off his head and brought it to David, foolishly expecting a reward. David, true to his principle that kings must not be harmed, had the two killed, and ordered that their horrific gift be buried in the fresh grave of Abner son of Ner.

Now there was no one remaining from among the house of Saul and his servants who could block the extension of David's rule over all Israel. As the sole sovereign of the land, David conquered Jerusalem and began to strengthen his monarchy, but he took care to fulfill his old promise to his friend Jonathan. Chapter 9 of Second Samuel opens with David's wish to find someone from the house of Saul to whom he might show kindness for Jonathan's sake. He found a servant of Saul's by the name of Ziba, and Ziba told him that Jonathan had a son called Mephibosheth, who lived in Lo-Debar, on the far side of the Jordan.

FROM THE BEGINNING OF HARVEST
UNTIL RAIN FELL

Mephibosheth was disabled. "He was five years old when the news of Saul and Jonathan came from Jezreel, and his nurse took him up, and fled; and it came to pass, as she made haste to flee, that he fell, and became lame."

"The news of Saul and Jonathan" was that the two had died, the grandfather and father of Mephibosheth, in the battle at the Gilboa. Now, after many years of suffering, disability, and orphanhood, Mephibosheth at last was granted a better fate. David ordered that he be given Saul's land and directed Ziba to work the fields and bring the produce to his master. He invited Mephibosheth to live in Jerusalem, and so it was: "Mephibosheth lived in Jerusalem; and he ate continually at the king's table; and he was lame in both feet."

It seems that Ziba was displeased with this arrangement. He waited for his moment, which came many years later, with the rebellion of David's son Absalom. David had then fled Jerusalem in fear of his son, and Ziba showed up with donkeys laden with provisions. When David asked where Mephibosheth was, Ziba said he had remained in Jerusalem, hoping that after the rebellion he would regain the portion of the kingdom that rightly belonged to his father Jonathan.

This made no sense. Why would Absalom give Mephibosheth half the kingdom he would win if his revolt was successful? David grew angry and said: "Then all that belongs to Mephibosheth is now yours!" And Ziba responded with his customary unctuousness: "I humbly beseech you that I may find grace in your sight, my lord, O king."

After Absalom's revolt, when the victorious David returned to Jerusalem, Mephibosheth came out to greet him. Now the truth came out. His servant Ziba had tricked him, and not saddled him a donkey to take him to David earlier. Owing to his lameness he was forced to stay home, where he sat and grieved, "and had neither dressed his feet, nor trimmed his beard, nor washed his clothes, from the day the king departed until the day he returned in peace." But by this time David was sick of all this. He decreed that Saul's land be divided between Mephibosheth and his servant, proving that already in biblical times, it paid to be a con man.

Chapter 21 of Second Samuel tells of the fate of the last members of the house of Saul. In this chapter, we read of a famine that afflicted the land after the revolt of Absalom. It is clear to the reader that this famine, like the rape of David's daughter Tamar by her half-brother Amnon, and the murder of Amnon by Absalom's men, and the revolt itself, was part of a series of punishments visited upon David for his sins in the Bathsheba affair, when he sent her husband Uriah to die in battle. But David inquired of God about the famine and was reassured by the Lord that it was because Saul had slain the Gibeonites. The Gibeonites were a small ethnic community living in the region of the tribe of Benjamin. They had deceived the Israelites during the period of conquest, pretending to be residents of a distant land. Joshua son of Nun had made a pact with them and promised they would not be harmed. When their deception was discovered, they were made into "hewers of wood and drawers of water" for the Israelites, the origin of an expression still in common use. They lived in their settlements in the lands of Benjamin, and the two peoples, unsurprisingly, did not get along.

David asked the Gibeonites what they wanted, and they said they wanted to kill seven of Saul's descendants. David agreed at once to hand them over. "I will do so," he said. Because of his oath to Jonathan he spared his son Mephibosheth, but he managed to forget that he had made the same oath to Saul as well. Saul had asked of David: "Swear now therefore to me by the Lord, that you will not cut off my seed after me," and David swore. Nevertheless, he now took the two sons that Rizpah the daughter of Aiah had borne to Saul, and the five sons that Michal the daughter of Saul had borne to Adriel the Meholathite, and gave them to the Gibeonites.

Who are these children? And who is Adriel the Meholathite? It was previously written that the second husband of Michal was Paltiel son of Laish. It turns out that Adriel is earlier mentioned as the husband of Merab, the older sister of Michal. I am, alas, unable to explain this mixup. Many commentators and scholars have tried to resolve it, but the matter remains a mystery. Apparently it is a remnant of various versions of the same stories.

In any event, the Gibeonites slew the seven descendants of Saul in the springtime, and left their bodies outdoors for display. "Then Rizpah the daughter of Aiah took sackcloth, and spread it on a rock for herself, and stayed there from the beginning of harvest until rain fell on them from the heavens; she did not allow the birds of the air to come on the bodies by day, or the wild animals by night." In other words, the poor mother made herself a little tent of sorts next to the bodies of her sons, and stayed there from the spring until the end of autumn, protecting them from the fangs of jackals and hyenas and the beaks of vultures.

When David heard of this, he commanded that the bones of Saul and Jonathan, which the men of Jabesh-Gilead had taken from the wall of Beth-Shean, be brought to him, and also the bones of Saul's offspring, whom he himself had handed over to the Gibeonites, and he had them all buried together in the burial plot of Kish, father of Saul, in the lands of Benjamin.

Thus came to an end the house of Saul, the first king of Israel. Not with an act of grace, but with another horror story. The saga that began with the awful tale of the Levite's concubine, raped and murdered at Gibeah in the region of Benjamin, ended with the terrible mistreatment of another concubine, whose sons were taken away from her by David and delivered into the murderous hands of the Gibeonites. There is no doubt that the second king of Israel was much better suited for the job than the first king.

THE FIRST WEEPING

*Abraham rose early in the morning, and took bread
and a skin of water, and gave them to Hagar. He placed
them over her shoulder, along with the child, and sent
her away. And she wandered about in the wilderness of
Beer-sheba. When the water in the skin was gone, she
left the child under one of the bushes. Then she went
and sat down opposite him a good way off, about the
distance of a bowshot; for she said, "Do not let me look
on the death of the child." And as she sat opposite him,
she lifted up her voice and wept. (Genesis 21)*

This desperate, alarming flood of tears, the weeping of
Hagar, is the first one in the Bible. The first tear is her
tear, and of all the tears of the oppressed that are chron-
icled in its pages, none compares with hers. The biblical author
who described the expulsion of Hagar and her son is a represen-
tative of the Jewish side of the family, the progeny of our father

Isaac, son of our mother Sarah. Yet he had the requisite honesty and sensitivity to award the first tears to Hagar. Indeed, his skillful rendering of Hagar's weeping, as concise and matter-of-fact as many other biblical descriptions, breaks the reader's heart today, after thousands of years.

When Sarah demanded, "cast out this slave and her son," it was very distressing to Abraham. But God said to him: "Let it not be grievous in your sight because of the lad, and because of your slave. Whatever Sarah tells you, do as she says; for it is through Isaac that offspring shall be continued for you."

God operates within an enormous time frame, and the event described here is but one step in his master plan. It could be that he took advantage of Sarah's animosity toward Hagar and Ishmael, in order to compel Abraham to choose the son who suited his program. "It is through Isaac that offspring shall be continued for you," God promised him, adding that Ishmael too would give rise to a great nation. But from Abraham's perspective all this talk is beside the point. The nations that will spring from his loins are not what concern him at the moment, but rather the fate of his son Ishmael, and I would imagine the fate of Hagar, his son's mother, as well.

But Abraham obeyed. Again, he obeyed. Abraham always obeys: he goes when he is told to go, circumcises himself when told to do so, banishes his son when this is demanded, binds his son for sacrifice when commanded to bind him. Abraham is the believer every god would wish for himself.

THE SON OF THIS SLAVE

A braham rose early in the morning, and took bread and a skin of water, and gave them to Hagar. He placed them over her shoulder, along with the child, and sent her away."

This child has a name. His name is Ishmael, and he has already been mentioned by name in the biblical text any number of times. But from the moment that God collaborated with Sarah in the matter of his banishment, the biblical author took the same position, and adopted the linguistic policy of Sarah, who said: "Cast out this slave and her son; for the son of this slave shall not be heir with my son, with Isaac."

From Sarah's standpoint, Hagar and Ishmael have no names, identities, or importance. Hagar is "this slave," Ishmael is "the son of this slave," and only her own son has a name, which she stresses with pride: "With my son, with Isaac." Yet she is not the only one who talks this way. God also adopts her wording: "Let it not be grievous in your sight because of the lad, and because of your slave. Whatever Sarah tells you, do as she says; for it is through Isaac that offspring shall be continued for you. And also of the son of the slave will I make a nation, because he is your seed."

Even on God's lips, Sarah and Isaac are Sarah and Isaac, while Hagar is the "slave" and Ishmael is "the lad" and "the son of the slave." And thus it will be throughout the chapter of the banishment. The name "Ishmael" will be replaced by "son of Hagar the Egyptian" and "son of the slave" and "the boy" and "the lad," as if God, Sarah, and the biblical author had all agreed that he has no name and identity, status and rights.

These stylistic nuances are not limited to the mention or omission of names. The sentence I cited above, "Abraham rose early in the morning," which begins the story of Ishmael's expulsion, fills an important role, as it recurs in the next chapter, Genesis 22, where it introduces an act of Abraham's that is even worse, the binding of Isaac: "Abraham rose early in the morning, saddled his donkey, and took two of his servants with him,

· and his son Isaac. He split the wood for the burnt offering, and set out and went to the place of which God had told him."

In both instances the same father got up early, and in both he did so in order to perform a horrifying act, not on his initiative and indeed against his will. In both stories, an angel of the Lord will appear and save the son's life at the last moment. In the case of Ishmael, water will be discovered as he is dying of thirst, and in Isaac's case, a ram appears, its horns caught in a thicket, to be sacrificed in his stead. But the important thing here is the behavior of Abraham, who in both instances acceded to God's dreadful demands without objection or debate. I would not be surprised if his willingness to banish Ishmael encouraged God to demand that he sacrifice Isaac in the following chapter. It's as if God wondered just how far this father's obedience would go, and what else he would be prepared to do.

I have already noted the biblical author's economy of language in telling the story of Isaac's binding. He is able to convey the turmoil in Abraham's soul without actually describing it. The minimalist prose and inner turmoil are also to be found in the chapter on the expulsion of Ishmael. Here too a full picture emerges from a few words: Abraham took the bread and water and "gave them to Hagar, and placed them over her shoulder." The reader can visualize how Abraham handed her the provisions, his eyes looking everywhere except into her eyes, and how she, frozen, aware of the cruel decree, refuses to take them, because to take them would mean participating in this evil plan that had been concocted against her and Ishmael.

And because Hagar refused to comply and did not take the provisions, Abraham set the pack on her shoulder, like putting something on a clothes hanger, or in a saddlebag. And he also gave her "the child"—whose name, in case anyone has

forgotten, is Ishmael, son of this man who is banishing him to
the desert. He gave him to her, because Hagar did not take him
either—and maybe, for all we know, Ishmael had been clinging
to his father the whole time.

And Sarah? Where was she while this was going on? Apparently she was in the tent, listening, just as she did when the angels came to Abraham with the news that Isaac would be born to
them. And who knows, maybe now too she was laughing inside.

FOR WE ARE KINSMEN

Abraham's obedience, here and in the binding of Isaac,
arouses astonishment and curiosity. It is customarily ascribed to his deep faith, and considered worthy of praise, but it
seems also to derive from an essential feature of his personality:
an aversion to confrontation. When a dispute broke out between
his shepherds and those of his nephew Lot, he parted ways from
him at once. It was a generous, peace-seeking separation, but the
fear of conflict was also obvious: "Let there be no strife between
you and me, and between your herders and my herders; for we
are kinsmen. Is not the whole land before you? Let us separate: If
you take the left hand, then I will go to the right; or if you take
the right hand, then I will go to the left."

So too when he went to Egypt and to the land of the Philistines. Abraham feared that the local kings would lust after his
pretty wife and kill him and take her, so he presented her as his
sister. But with all due respect to Sarah's good looks, it may be
assumed that Abraham was not the only married man to arrive
in a foreign land, and I find it hard to believe that all the other
husbands who encountered Abimelech of Gerar or the pharaoh
of Egypt acted the same way.

In the aforementioned clash between Sarah and Hagar, he

acted the same way. Sarah claimed that her slave-woman, from the moment she got pregnant, looked down on her, and that complaint was indeed justified. But Abraham, instead of putting Hagar in her place, again took the easy way out: "Your maid is in your hands. Deal with her as you think right," he said to his wife, and Sarah treated Hagar so abusively that she ran away.

In fact, apart from his pursuit of the kings who had abducted Lot, Abraham did not come into conflict with anyone. Even in his conversation with God about the number of righteous men needed to save Sodom from destruction, the same behavior pattern applies. On the surface, Abraham argued vigorously and even challenged the Lord: "Shall not the Judge of all the earth do what is just?" Yet this debate, too, reflects the same hesitancy. Instead of asking God to spare his beloved nephew Lot, like many a good Jew who has made requests of the Almighty, Abraham went round and round in a tedious analysis of reward and punishment.

Above it all hovers the question of the fate of his two sons. Abraham argued over the fate of the righteous men of Sodom, of whom there were none, except Lot. But over the lives of Ishmael and Isaac he argued not at all. In both cases he succumbed to demands and instructions, his wife's and God's. He sent Ishmael into the desert and bound Isaac on the altar. Unfortunately, the man designated to be the "father of many nations" failed as the father of his two sons.

BLESS ME TOO, FATHER

The second weeping in the Bible is that of Esau. He cried when he realized that his brother and mother had tricked his father into giving Jacob the blessing that was intended for him. Ostensibly, Jacob and Rebecca took advantage of Isaac's blindness. But in fact they also relied on his unquenchable passion for fine food. Earlier in the text it is written that Isaac loved Esau "because he had a taste for game," because Esau cooked him delicious meat. And his request that Esau hunt and fix him savory food "that my soul may bless you before I die" attests to tremendous desire bordering on hysteria, since Isaac lived many years after that particular meal.

At first glance, Esau's weeping makes less sense than Hagar's. She and her son had been sent into the desert, where they faced a life-threatening situation. Esau had not been banished anywhere. He was a grown man, fully independent, and not a helpless woman or child. But there is also a similarity between the two cases of weeping, stemming from the similarity between Esau and Ishmael, and the attitude of the patriarchs toward them. Both were hunters, outdoorsmen. Ishmael grew up to be "an archer," and Esau sought prey with his "quiver and bow." Both were elder brothers who were dismissed and deposed, stripped of their birthright and role in the family's history.

Esau's weeping was preceded by a cry. When he returned from the hunt and discovered that Jacob had received the blessing meant for him, he cried "with a great and very bitter cry." A cry without words, bespeaking anger and distress. For a moment it seemed that his bitterness was released together with his cry, and he would now calm down. He even tried to find a solution to the situation. "Bless me, me too, father," he asked of Isaac. But Isaac said that all the good blessings had already been given away to Jacob, "and what, then, can I still do for you, my son?"

Only now does Esau comprehend what has happened. "Have you but one blessing, father? Bless me, me too, father!" His tone shifts in mid-sentence, from anger to criticism to pleading, and the repetition of the word "me" indicates that even as he is speaking Esau is coming to understand the real significance of the matter, that his father is the only one he can turn to, not his mother, for he is no longer her son. And without waiting for his father's reply, he breaks down: "Esau lifted up his voice, and wept." He weeps not over the lost blessing. He weeps because his own mother has betrayed him, it was she and no one else who has plotted against him, as Sarah had done to Ishmael.

I imagine this was an awful spectacle. Esau, the brawny, hairy hunter, the bold and mighty outdoorsman, broke down and cried like a baby. We shall not find him crying again until many years later, at his next meeting with Jacob, their reconciliation. For now, Jacob will flee to Haran to escape his brother's likely vengeance, and Esau—how natural and predictable and touching—will go to the man who resembles him most, the family's previous banished brother, Uncle Ishmael. He will go to him, and even take his daughter for a wife.

HE LIFTED UP HIS VOICE AND WEPT

The next weeping is heard several weeks later, and many miles away, at a well in Kedem, the land to the east. Jacob, who fled his brother's wrath, crossed the desert, arrived in Haran, and burst into tears when he first saw Rachel. These are not tears of sorrow or distress, but the opposite. These are the happiest and most surprising tears in the Bible.

The events are recounted in Genesis 29: "When Jacob saw Rachel, the daughter of his mother's brother Laban, and the sheep of his mother's brother Laban, Jacob went up and rolled the stone from the mouth of the well, and watered the flock of his mother's brother Laban. Then Jacob kissed Rachel, and lifted up his voice and wept . . . And Jacob told Rachel that he was her father's kinsman, and that he was Rebecca's son."

At first glance it seems that Jacob was confused by excitement, since he handled this initial meeting in an odd way. His last action, introducing himself as Rachel's cousin, should have come first, certainly before that bold and unexpected kiss. But on second thought, even if he ran afoul of convention and propriety, he acted with intelligence and calculation: Jacob sought to impress Rachel as a man, not a relative. As a stranger, he showed his strength and chivalry, passion and daring. His taking notice of "the sheep of his mother's brother Laban" is another sign of careful thinking. Jacob also evaluated the situation from a practical angle, and was pleased to see that his uncle owned an impressive flock, which would provide him with work and an income.

Amid this rational performance, only Jacob's weeping was not planned ahead of time. He burst into tears in a flood of emotion, and I dare to speculate that he surprised even himself. This may have turned out to be his most effective means of courting Rachel. For strong men who can roll stones from the mouths of wells are many in number. And chivalrous gentlemen who offer to water the sheep of a pretty young woman are not lacking either. And smart-alecks who would kiss her without permission—of these, alas, there are plenty, then as now. But as for a young man who would meet a girl for the first time, take one look at her and burst into tears, there is only one: Jacob. His weeping is out of love and emotion, in contrast not only with the angry and anguished weeping of Esau, but also with Jacob's failure to cry on other occasions, past and future: when he says good-bye to his mother, when Rachel dies, when he thinks that Joseph has been torn apart by wild beasts, and when he meets him again in Egypt, where Joseph is second in command to the pharaoh.

Indeed, crying that did not occur is also of interest to readers of the Bible. Abraham laughed when God gave him the news that Isaac would be born, but he did not cry when God commanded him to sacrifice him on the altar. David and Jonathan wept when they were compelled to part, but David and Michal did not. And in one instance we are given an explanation, both of weeping and its absence: when God visited illness upon the firstborn child of David and Bathsheba, the king fasted and cried. But when the child died, David rose, washed, and changed his clothes.

His servants asked of him: "What thing is this that you have done? While the child was alive, you fasted and wept; but now that the child is dead, you rise and eat food?"

And David answered: "While the child was still alive, I fasted and wept; for I said, 'Who knows? The Lord may have pity on me, and the child may live.' But now he is dead; why should I fast? Can I bring him back again? I shall go to him, but he will never come back to me."

Weeping is not only an involuntary response to sorrow, pain, or emotion; it is also a practical, demonstrative action, designed to arouse the attention and sympathy of others. In this case, David directed his weeping at God, but in another instance he directed it at the entire nation, when he wept at the funeral of Abner son of Ner, who was killed by Joab in Hebron. As noted in the previous chapter, David's weeping over Abner did not spring from sorrow, but was intended to make clear to the people that he was not responsible for Abner's death. The scene is described in Second Samuel 3, and readers will find that David achieved his purpose.

Only over his son Absalom, also slain by Joab, did David

genuinely weep, shedding tears that contradicted his explanation at the death of the child borne him by Bathsheba. This weeping was not meant to restore his dead son Absalom to the land of the living, nor to arouse the attention of others, but rather uncontrollable weeping, honest and true, ignoring the fact that Absalom was a rebellious son who not only sought his father's crown but wanted to kill him. Indeed, Joab was impelled to remind David that he was not only a bereaved father but a king who had quashed a dangerous rebellion. He demanded that he stop crying and go before the people, lest his followers abandon him, and David overcame his sorrow and did just that.

DAVID WEPT LONGER

If we tally all the weeping ascribed to the heroes of Scripture, it appears that Joseph and David are the two great criers of the Bible, and perhaps of the Jewish people in general. This is interesting, because there is another similarity between the two: they were both beloved, smart, and creative. Both were strikingly good-looking men whose pretty faces gave no hint of their inner strength.

And not only that. Both were little brothers disliked by their older ones, who spoke of them with mockery and even hatred. Both were sent by their fathers to see how their older brothers were faring. David was sent to the battlefield in the Valley of Elah, where his brothers were fighting with the Israelite army against the Philistines. His brothers were unwelcoming, but he defeated Goliath and in the end became king of Israel. Joseph was sent to his brothers who were grazing their flocks in the Valley of Dothan. They attacked him and sold him to Ishmaelites; but after enslavement and jail time, he became Pharaoh's viceroy.

Another point of similarity is worth noting: when the two rose to greatness they didn't provide jobs to their brothers. Joseph hosted and housed his brothers in Egypt, but he didn't give them government jobs. David embraced and promoted Joab and Abishai, the sons of his sister Zeruiah, but not his older brothers, who had not treated him nicely when he was young. One may imagine that as the youngest brother, the handsome and unusual one, he was closer to his sister than to his brothers. There is no basis for this in the narrative itself, but this is one of the Bible's greatest qualities—its capacity to prompt us to weave new stories within and around it.

Both men, Joseph and David, managed and led countries. But Joseph did so in a foreign land, and David in his own land. Joseph ran the economy; David excelled mainly in the military arena. Both were attractive to women, but Joseph controlled his urges whereas David succumbed to his. Here we touch upon the biggest difference between them: Joseph underwent a positive metamorphosis, from a spoiled and arrogant youth to a person who utilized his talents for the good of society at large. David's metamorphosis was negative. He was as good-looking and intelligent as Joseph, but his charm and accomplishments ruined his moral judgment. He committed the sin that Joseph avoided, after which he declined into a miserable and premature old age.

As for their crying—David wept in various circumstances and periods in his life, and his tears were parceled among years and causes, while Joseph wept in the course of one event: his reunion with his family. The Bible does not specify whether he cried when his mother died, when he was thrown into the pit, or when he was imprisoned for a crime he did not commit. The text tells only of his tears that began when his brothers came to Egypt to buy grain.

At the outset of their first encounter Joseph showed great self-control. His brothers did not recognize him but he recognized them, and managed to conceal this. He kept aloof from them and spoke harshly. He even claimed they were spies and ordered them thrown in jail. But when he heard them talking among themselves—unaware that the Egyptian viceroy could understand their language—about their guilt, their sale of Joseph to the Ishmaelites, his unheeded pleas for mercy on that awful day, he could not contain himself, and went off to cry where no one could see him.

Joseph wept again when the brothers, at his command, brought Benjamin to him. Now that the dam of his tears had burst at their earlier meeting, and because his little brother, son of the same mother, now stood before him, he cried right away. The Bible stresses how quickly this happened: "Joseph hurried out, because he was overcome with feeling for his brother, and was on the verge of tears. So he went into a private room and wept there." But then he washed his face and returned to his brothers, without revealing his secret.

Only the next day, when the silver goblet planted by Joseph was found in Benjamin's sack of grain, and Judah told him, as if talking to a stranger, that he, Joseph, was dead, and that Jacob would likely die if anything bad happened to Benjamin too—Joseph could no longer hold back. He cleared the room of his attendants so he could make himself known to his brothers in private, but when he started to cry, it was a big cry: "And he wept so loudly that the Egyptians heard it, and the household of Pharaoh heard it."

After many years of restraint, Joseph could restrain himself no more. He could no longer be estranged from his brothers, nor from himself. He gave free rein to his feelings, and broke out in tears. At the conclusion of this meeting Joseph hugged Benjamin, and they each wept on the other's neck. Then he kissed all his brothers and wept on each of their necks too.

We shall return to Joseph and his brothers, in our chapter called "The First Hate." For now I will cite one more of his crying episodes, which occurred when his father Jacob came to Egypt: "Joseph made ready his chariot and went up to meet his father Israel in Goshen. He presented himself to him, fell on his neck, and wept on his neck a good while." Later, he wept when his father died, and his last weeping came when his brothers, who feared his revenge, made up a story, claiming that Jacob on his deathbed had asked Joseph to forgive them of their sin.

As I have mentioned, David also cried many tears. He cried when parting from Jonathan, where the text specifies that they "wept one with another; David wept longer." He wept with all his men—"until they had no more strength to weep"—when the Philistines overran them and made off with their women and children. This weeping, by the way, did not interfere with running after the captors, smiting them by sword, and rescuing their loved ones. He wept when Saul and Jonathan died, slain on the Gilboa. He cried an unusual cry, as previously noted, at the funeral of Abner son of Ner. He cried when his firstborn son by Bathsheba became mortally ill, and stopped crying when the child died. Thrice more David cried, because of his son Absalom. He "wept very bitterly" when Absalom murdered his other son Amnon, and wept when he was forced to flee Jerusalem when Absalom rebelled against him, and cried again when Absalom was dead.

I remarked earlier that this last weeping by David is the only one that touches the reader's heart, and not just because it is genuine, but because the author added a few perfect words that cannot leave us indifferent: "My son, Absalom my son, my son Absalom, if only I had died instead of you, Absalom, my son, my son . . ."

I'm not sure that's the right punctuation. I could read: "My son Absalom. My son, my son Absalom. If only I had died instead of you, Absalom. My son . . . My son." Other configurations are possible. In all of them the writing simulates a blend of weeping and speech, and the reader mumbles the words to himself, imagining the breaths and sobs and pauses, the swallowing of saliva, and inserts the commas accordingly. So too with David's next cry, a few verses later: "My son Absalom Absalom my son my son."

It may well be that David's mystique, which endures to this day, is a product of his astounding diversity, his ability to play the lyre, kill Goliath, rule over Israel, commit adultery, slay the lion and bear, write poetry, gather Philistine foreskins, murder, and weep.

One more weeping must be credited to David, though not his own. This is the weeping of Paltiel son of Laish, the second husband of Michal, the daughter of Saul. Of all the crying men in the Bible—of whom, it turns out, there were many—he is the one whose tears most touch my heart.

WEEPING AS HE WALKED

It will be recalled that Michal, daughter of Saul, was David's first wife. After David escaped the royal palace with her help, her father gave her to Paltiel son of Laish from Galim. I do not know how this was legally possible, but it is likely that in those days kings were not much bothered by legal niceties the way we are today. In any event, after Saul died, when David crowned himself in Hebron, he was quick to order Abner son of Ner,

Saul's military chief, and Ish-Bosheth, Saul's son, to bring Michal back to him.

"Ish-Bosheth sent and took her from her husband Paltiel son of Laish. But her husband went with her, weeping as he walked behind her all the way to Bahurim. Then Abner said to him, 'Go back home!' So he went back."

Galim, which is also mentioned in the book of Isaiah, was then located in the territory of the tribe of Benjamin, northeast of Jerusalem, near Anathoth. Bahurim, also mentioned in the story of Absalom's rebellion, was just east of Jerusalem. Thus Paltiel walked a few miles southward, following Michal, "weeping as he walked," until commanded to return home, which he did.

Every time I arrive at this verse I muse about its characters, its syntax and meter, and the author who composed it. We know nothing at all about Paltiel son of Laish, except that Saul gave him Michal, David's wife, and that when David demanded her return, he walked after her weeping till Bahurim. Apparently he was a Benjaminite, judging by his place of residence and his connection with Saul. But it is not known if he was a shepherd or planter, woodworker or cloth merchant, old or young. Was Michal his only wife, or did he have others? Whatever the case, just as Joshua has gone down in history as conqueror of the Land, and Solomon is remembered as the wisest of men, Paltiel son of Laish is the man who walked weeping after his stolen wife all the way to Bahurim. The reader, if he has any heart, weeps with him, and in the way of great literature, not just because of the story but also the way it is written.

The literal Hebrew for Paltiel's "walking and weeping," *halokh u'vakho*, is a strong and precise construction with parallels elsewhere in the Bible. When Samson, in the book of Judges, scooped honey from the carcass of the lion he had slain, he ate it while walking, *vayelekh halokh v'akhol*. The cows that pulled the cart carrying the Ark of God away from Philistine territory, in First Samuel 6, were mooing as they walked, *halokh v'ga'o*. So too when the flood waters in Genesis 8 "went on diminishing," *halokh v'hasor*—another description of an ongoing, and perhaps intensifying, activity.

I draw myself a mental picture: Abner rides at the head of the small caravan, spear in hand, the same spear with which he killed Asahel son of Zeruiah. Now and again, when the mountain trail widens or splits temporarily, he pulls back and rides alongside. Michal, sitting straight-backed in silence—I always imagine her with a straight back—rides behind Abner, on a female mule sent by David for the purpose. Do not look for this mule in the Bible; it is not mentioned. But certainly it is there, and it is no ordinary mule. David would not let Michal ride on just any animal, would certainly not let her make the journey on foot; he demanded that she be returned to him because she was the daughter of a king and would now be a king's wife. A woman like this must ride on a fine-looking mule from the royal stables.

Several soldiers and cavalrymen protect Michal, and, in the rear, at a distance that expands and, contracts in accordance with nods from Abner, walks Paltiel, the husband who was robbed. He does not dare try to touch her, or come close, or even look at her for too long. Everyone is silent. The mission is unpleasant for all concerned. Only two sounds can be heard. The incessant, muffled crying of Paltiel, and the hooves of horses and mules on the rocky ground, sharp and pleasant to the ear.

There is so much love here, and shamelessness, and helplessness too, and not one word spoken about Michal herself, who knows she has been taken from a man who loves her more

than any man ever loved a woman in the Bible, and is being returned to a man who never loved her and will not love her now.
To David, whom she loved before, and maybe still does.

She sits very straight and does not turn her head or utter a
sound. Not a word, not a sigh, not a sob of her own.

"Go back home!" commands Abner.

And she does not see Paltiel stop, does not sense his final
gaze, which quivers on her back like sunlight in a mirror, and
does not turn her head when he turns around and walks away,
toward their home. An entire novel is hidden here, compressed
into a single biblical verse, which opens up and tells its tale to an
empathetic reader.

THE FIRST SPIES

The first profession mentioned in the Bible is that of Abel, a shepherd. Immediately thereafter, in the same verse, Genesis 4:2, the first farmer appears—his brother Cain. After these two, toward the end of the same chapter, come the first breeder of livestock, musician, and blacksmith: Jabal, "the father of those who live in tents and have cattle"; Jubal, "the father of all who play the lyre and pipe"; and Tubal-Cain, "forger of implements of copper and iron." The two latter figures have special significance, as they were endowed with knowledge, creativity, and inventiveness that their predecessors lacked. They were the first to go beyond the dreary subsistence described in the first chapter of Genesis: the domination and consumption of animals and plants. Tubal-Cain was the father of human technology and Jubal was the first artist—a musician—and both energized mankind with the capacity to rise above the primitive existence bestowed by the Creator.

After the great flood came the first hunter, Nimrod, and

the first builders, who erected the Tower of Babel. Upon Abraham's visit to Egypt, mention is made of another indispensable profession—royal courtiers—and, later on in the book of Genesis, the oldest profession: prostitution. The word "prostitute" first appears in connection with Jacob's daughter Dinah, and thereafter with Tamar, the wife of Er; and so as not to sully their good name, let me emphasize that neither of them was a whore. Dinah's brothers, avenging her rape by Shechem son of Hamor, said: "Should our sister be treated like a whore?" Tamar masqueraded as a harlot, in order to seduce her father-in-law Judah and become pregnant by him.

With the sale of Joseph to the Ishmaelites we meet the first merchants, and later, in Egypt, there are all manner of bureaucrats, magicians, and advisers. Joseph is made the viceroy of the Egyptian king, and it was he who first made mention of the line of work I now wish to discuss: espionage.

"You are spies!" he accused his brothers, who had come to Egypt to buy grain. "To see the nakedness of the land you have come!"

We learn from this that spying is a very old occupation, commonplace in the Middle East even in ancient times, and that the spies of yesteryear did exactly what spies do today: they secretly gathered information. Joseph's biblical Hebrew employs a fine metaphor—the spies come to "see the nakedness of the land," that is to say, to expose what must not be seen. In the Bible, seeing and exposing nakedness also refers to sexual contact, or "knowing," a word that obviously applies to espionage too. It appears in Second Samuel 3, when Joab son of Zeruiah also accuses a guest of spying. Joab claimed that Abner son of Ner's visit to Hebron to see David was intended "to know your going out and your coming in, and to know all that you do." In our own day the Hebrew root for knowing, *yda'*, has evolved into the drab *modi'in,* meaning "intelligence" as in "military intelligence," but it's nice to note the spicy etymology.

Espionage and counterespionage return in other contexts. The tribe of Dan, in Judges 18, sent five men of valor "to spy out the land and search it," to find themselves a territory to settle. In Second Samuel 10, the Ammonites suspected that a diplomatic delegation sent by David had come "to search the city, and to spy it out, and to overthrow it." David himself spied on Saul when the latter pursued him in the desert, and planted agents in Jerusalem to report to him as he fled his rebellious son Absalom. Better known than any of these were the two spies Joshua sent to Jericho, who hid in the home of Rahab the harlot, of whom we shall soon hear more.

But the most famous of all the spies in the Bible were the twelve sent by Moses from the wilderness of Paran to scout the land of Canaan. This episode of espionage is the best known of them all, and the most detailed, and also the biggest failure. Reading the account sheds light on professional aspects of spying, and also on the complicated relations between the political echelon and the operational echelon in all times and places.

SEND MEN

A nd the Lord spoke to Moses, saying: Send men, that they may spy the land of Canaan, which I give to the people of Israel."

So begins chapter 13 of the book of Numbers. The reader may well ask: What is the need for spies when the leader of the nation is a prophet? Why explore and investigate the land if God has already said that it flows with milk and honey? And why prepare for a war of conquest if God has already promised the land to the Israelites?

The Bible will furnish answers to all these questions. In the meantime, I ask the reader to make note of who initiated the sending of the spies, since later on, as is common in cases of this sort, there will be commissions of inquiry. And in the future, as happens after failures like these, the question will be asked: "Who gave the order?" It's therefore best that the answer be clear at the outset: God gave the order. He and none other. This is why I have just quoted from the opening of Numbers 13, and to be on the safe side, I will do it again: "And the Lord spoke to Moses, saying: Send men, that they may spy the land of Canaan, which I give to the people of Israel."

God did not stop at that. He also went into operational detail, instructing Moses to send the chieftains of the tribes, no less: "From each of their ancestral tribes you shall send a man, every one a leader among them." The text goes on to stress that these were "chiefs of the people of Israel" and were chosen and sent "by the commandment of the Lord." This emphasis is very important. If it had been a human being who had made the decision to send the tribal chieftains on an espionage mission, we would call it a mistake. But if God made the decision, who are we to second-guess him?

Thus was a band of men—inexperienced, too large, and too conspicuous—dispatched to the land of Canaan. Worst of all, they were a bunch of politicians, self-serving by nature, prone to grudge-holding, driven by conflicting interests, and endowed with more than a smidgen of competitiveness. Why did God choose them of all people? It seems to me that the story's author—who doubtless knew its bitter end—wanted the top political echelon of all the tribes to be involved in this future failure, so that each could share the responsibility.

Moses's directives to the spies attest that he too was no professional in the field of espionage: "Go up there into the Negeb, and on into the hill country, and see what the land is like, and whether the people who live in it are strong or weak, whether they are few or many, and whether the land they live in is good or bad, and whether the towns that they live in are unwalled or fortified, and whether the land is rich or poor, and whether there are trees in it or not. Be bold, and bring some of the fruit of the land."

The instructions are quite confusing. Moses begins with the quality of the land, moves on to the strength and number of the inhabitants, goes back to the land's quality, moves to the type of fortifications, then back to questions of quality and asks the spies to bring back fruit as proof of the land's fertility. This last request is strange and unprofessional, since it has no value as intelligence but is more for show, and constitutes a burden for the spies.

Moreover, one may again ask, why all the bother? Long before the spies were sent, back in Leviticus 26, God provided clear answers to these very questions. Concerning the quality of the land, he declared: "If you follow My statutes and faithfully observe My commandments, I will give you your rains in their season, and the land shall yield its produce, and the trees of the field shall yield their fruit. Your threshing shall last to the time of vintage, and the vintage shall last to the sowing time; you shall eat your bread to the full." In other words, if the Israelites obey God's laws, the land will be good and fat and bountiful. And if they don't listen to God's voice, the land will be lean: "Your land shall not yield her produce, nor shall the trees of the land yield their fruits."

As to gauging the military might of the inhabitants, no spies are necessary either. God already promised his people in Leviticus that if they believe in him and listen to his voice, they will win regardless of the strength of the locals: "You shall chase your enemies, and they shall fall before you by the sword." And if his people don't obey the commandments, they will be defeated: "You shall be struck down by your enemies, and your foes shall rule over you." In short, there is no reason to send spies to check if the land is fertile and if its cities are fortified and its residents strong. All the answers to all the questions are known in advance.

BETWEEN TWO ON A POLE

The departure of the spies thus arouses a fair degree of puzzlement, but their return is stranger still. In general, an agent who comes back from a mission is closeted with his handlers and debriefed in secret. Here, with astounding openness, the spies reported their findings to the entire nation: "And they came to Moses and Aaron and the whole Israelite community in the wilderness of Paran, at Kadesh; they brought back word to them and to the whole community, and showed them the fruit of the land."

The public venue of their reporting, along with the caliber of the delegation and the instructions to carry back and display the fruit of the land, lead the reader to suspect that the spies were not sent simply for intelligence gathering. Indeed the report and its consequences confirm this. First, the spies sang the land's praises and showed everyone its fruit—a cluster of grapes so big it had to be borne by two men on a pole. Then they listed by name all the peoples of the land and their locations, finally describing their military strength.

The people who dwell in the Promised Land, they said, are strong and mighty, and the cities are big and fortified, "and we even saw giants there, the descendants of Anak." Upon hearing these words, the crowd got scared and noisy. One of the spies, Caleb son of Jephunneh, chieftain of the tribe of Judah, hushed them with a patriotic verse that many patriots quote to this day: "Let us go up at once, and possess it, for we are well able to overcome it."

These words made the situation more difficult. The twelve spies had been asked to provide data, not practical evaluations. And for all the affection we have for proud Jews like Caleb, statements like his are supposed to come from the central command, not from the spy himself. From the minute Caleb exceeded his mandate and announced, "Let us go up at once, and possess it," the dam burst. The rest of the spies stopped presenting facts and started giving opinions, which were very different from his: "We are not able to go up against the people, for they are stronger than we," they said, adding that the land "is a land that eats up its inhabitants," and there are giants living in it, "and to ourselves we looked like grasshoppers, and so we must have looked to them."

Apart from the literary artistry exhibited here by the spies, and their fine entomological analogies, it must be noted that like Caleb son of Jephunneh, his colleagues who opposed him also forgot their assignment. They reverted to their political roles as chieftains of tribes, and weighed the issues faced by politicians. This was only natural. They stood before the entire nation and were concerned about their status and image, their own interests and those of their tribe.

In the case of Caleb son of Jephunneh, the matter was particularly significant. This man was the chief of the tribe of

Judah, and according to the spies' itinerary—"they went up into the Negeb, and came to Hebron"—it turns out that they mainly investigated the territory that would become the portion of Caleb's tribe, and from there they brought their famous cluster of grapes. It is altogether likely that this fact influenced his perceptions and brought about his quick shift from intelligence reporting to proclamations and slogans.

God, as well as the biblical author and generations of commentators, praised Caleb and denounced his opponents, but the public debate Caleb provoked frightened the Israelites and caused a collapse of morale. They were so fearful that they declared: " 'If only we had diedin the land of Egypt! Or if only we might die in this wilderness! Why is the Lord bringing us into this land to fall by the sword? Our wives and our little ones will become booty; would it not be better for us to go back to Egypt?' So they said to one another, 'Let us choose a captain, and go back to Egypt.' "

At the sight of such defeatism, which could have cost him his tribal portion, Caleb son of Jephunneh redoubled his resolve. This time he was joined by Joshua son of Nun, also no ordinary spy, but the man who would one day inherit the mantle of Moses. He too had his own considerations, not to mention the agenda of the author who described him.

The two men tore their clothes as a sign of mourning and said: "The land that we traversed and scouted is an exceedingly good land. If the Lord is pleased with us, He will bring us into this land and give it to us, a land that flows with milk and honey. Only, do not rebel against the Lord; and do not fear the people of the land, for they are our prey; their protection has departed from them, but the Lord is with us; do not fear them."

The words are fine and inspiring, and they tone down the

demagoguery of Caleb's "let us go up and possess it for we can overcome it," but there is nothing new here. The beginning is exactly the same as what the other ten spies had said, that the land is good and fertile, and what follows—"the Lord is with us; do not fear them"—is identical to what has already been said many times in the Torah, for instance, in the passage in Leviticus where it says that if the Israelites obey the Lord, he will give them the land and subdue its inhabitants. This being the case, it may again be asked, why send spies in the first place? And why hear their report now? And why lug a huge cluster of grapes from Hebron to the wilderness of Paran? Indeed, upon hearing the words of Caleb and Joshua, the Israelites wanted to stone them. That's how bad things got.

In the annals of the Jews, this episode is ranked one of the most painful, and it is surely the most serious of the traumas suffered by the Israelies in the desert. The spies who slandered the land—this is how the text defines the ones who opposed Joshua and Caleb—are stigmatized as the worst sort of our people. But if the reader checks the facts, and, unlike the spies, does not offer opinions, he will find that not only they were to blame. This is what happens when nonprofessional spies are sent out with unclear orders and then deliver their findings to the entire nation.

But all this is trivial compared with the strange behavior ascribed by the author to God, who was quick to make a show of anger and umbrage. "How long will these people despise Me? And how long will they refuse to believe in Me, in spite of all the signs that I have done among them?" God complained to Moses. In other words: after all the signs, all the miracles I have performed in their behalf, these ingrates still doubt my power.

Not all the authors of the Bible were equally talented and wise. More than once, God falls victim to the clumsy prose of a mediocre writer, and this is one of the more unfortunate examples. God is presented here as an insulted grouch. He is sick and tired of skepticism concerning his capabilities, disgusted by the doubts over his signs and wonders and miracles. The humiliation is so deep that the author even has God declare to Moses his intention to wipe out the whole people at once, and establish a new nation from the leader's own seed!

Luckily, and amazingly enough, that same author attributes to Moses greater discretion, logic, and maturity than he ascribes to the Master of the Universe. Moses did not join in the Almighty's outrage, and he even explained matters to the Lord in a curious way: The destruction of the Israelites will merely damage God's image. Other nations will say that God destroyed his people because he lacked the ability to bring them to the Promised Land: "It is because the Lord was powerless to bring this people into the land He swore to give them that He has slaughtered them in the wilderness."

This is not the first time that such an argument was brought to bear upon God. A similar debate took place following the incident of the golden calf. There too, God toyed with the idea of destroying the Children of Israel and founding a new chosen people out of Moses's seed, and there too Moses responded: "Let not the Egyptians say, 'It was with evil intent that He delivered them, only to kill them off in the mountains and annihilate them from the face of the earth.' "

In both these instances Moses hit home, with a precise reading of God's mental state and his concern over his image and honor. And in both cases God revealed his great sensitivity to public relations and world opinion. Both times, God overcame the "stop me before I do something rash" mode imposed by the author, and speedily reversed his decision.

"I forgive, as you have asked," God said to Moses, but did not forget to add that the Lord's presence would fill the whole world, and all those who doubted it would not reach the land of Israel, the exceptions being Joshua son of Nun and Caleb son of Jephunneh. Caleb, he emphasized, would receive the territory he explored, "because he had another spirit with him, and has followed me fully, him will I bring into the land where he went; and his seed shall possess it."

HE HAS FOLLOWED ME FULLY

At first reading, it seems that the key words in the verse are "another spirit," but this isn't so. The truly important phrase is "followed me fully," which means, "confirmed what I said." These words settle all the apprehensions the reader felt regarding this espionage mission from the outset. They indicate that God did not praise Caleb for his reliable and precise intelligence work, nor for his courage and devotion to the task. He praised him because his report confirmed what God himself had said about the Promised Land. This also makes clear why God had commanded that the spies bring back fruit of the land, which resulted in their carrying those grapes from Hebron. The reconnaissance assignment actually had nothing to do with the conquest of the land, its armies and fortifications. It was meant to verify and confirm God's promises that the land was good and fat, flowing with milk and honey.

Interestingly, the expression "to follow God fully" is used again by Caleb himself many years later, in Joshua 14. On the eve of the apportionment of the land among the tribes, Caleb turned to Joshua son of Nun and reminded him of the spying episode in which they had both taken part. "I was forty years old when Moses the servant of the Lord sent me from Kadesh-barnea to spy out the land; and I brought him an honest report. But my companions who went up with me made the heart of the people fail; yet I fully followed the Lord my God." He even quoted Moses's promise from that time: "The land on which your foot trod shall be an inheritance for you and your descendants forever, because you have fully followed the Lord my God."

In a dramatic finish, Caleb asked Joshua to fulfill the promise of Moses: "And now, here I am today, eighty-five years old. I am still as strong today as I was on the day that Moses sent me; my strength now is as my strength was then, for war, and for going and coming. So now give me this hill country of which the Lord spoke on that day."

Biblical scholars are better qualified than I am to analyze the historical background of the story of the spies. Did it happen, or not? And if it did, does it perhaps camouflage a separate story about the conquest and settlement of the tribe of Judah, similar to the story later on of the tribes who settled east of the Jordan? Or does it hint at a narrative of some other attempt at settlement, which ended in defeat? Unfortunately, I lack the scholarly tools to probe these questions in depth. But the phrase that repeats itself in connection with Caleb, that he "followed God fully," proves God's true goal in ordering Moses to send out the spies: not strategy, but image. Not to bring back facts and figures, but to confirm to the Israelites the truth of the promises God had made to them as they wandered in the desert. This might make the reader uneasy, because generally the situation is reversed: man seeks proofs and signs and confirmations from God, not the other way around.

GO UP, TAKE POSSESSION

As I have noted, Moses was the only one who stayed cool and logical, but he too was unable to forget the episode. Forty years thereafter, on the eve of Israel's entering the Promised Land, he again brought it up. This is recounted in Numbers 32, where the tribes of Gad and Reuben and half the tribe of Manasseh seek to settle on the eastern side of the Jordan, in the territory promised to them, and not to participate in the conquest of the western land of Israel with the other tribes.

Moses became angry: "Shall your brothers go to war while you stay here? Why will you discourage the hearts of the Israelites from crossing over into the land that the Lord has given them? This is what your fathers did, when I sent them from Kadesh-barnea to survey the land. When they went up to the Wadi Eshcol and saw the land, they discouraged the hearts of the Israelites from going into the land that the Lord had given them."

In his rage, Moses dubbed the members of the spies' generation "a breed of sinful men." The biblical Hebrew here for "breed" (or "brood," in some translations) is *tarbut*, which appears nowhere else in the Bible and in modern Hebrew means "culture." Moses again praised Caleb and Joshua, using the familiar expression, "for they followed the Lord fully." The wording and tone make it clear that the episode of the spies was neither forgotten nor forgiven. It is worth noting another detail: Moses rewrote a small but significant bit of the original story. He repeated what had earlier been written, that he had sent out the spies, but omitted the fact that God had told him to do so.

Several chapters later, in the first chapter of Deuteronomy, we find a greater and more significant revision of the whole affair. As the Israelites were about to enter the land, Moses provided them an account of all that had happened between the Exodus from Egypt and the present date. In the book of Numbers, the story is told in the third person, as the report of the biblical author, but the version in Deuteronomy is first-person, as a subsequent report of Moses himself. The biblical author thus puts words in the mouth of Moses—the most important mouth in the Bible—that are of great importance to the author himself.

The story of the spies according to Moses, a new and cleaner version, appears in Deuteronomy 1. As opposed to the account in Numbers, where God said to send spies and Moses did what God ordered, Moses now says that he never intended to send spies, but rather urged the people to go and conquer the land right away: "See, the Lord your God has given the land to you; go up, take possession, as the Lord, the God of your fathers, has promised you; do not fear or be dismayed."

Interesting. Moses's "go up, take possession"—*aleh resh* in the terse Hebrew—recalls Caleb's words in Numbers 13, "Let us go up at once, and possess it." Apparently, the author of Deuteronomy knew the version of the story in Numbers, and so his Moses adopts the bold stance of Caleb. But now comes the big surprise of the Deuteronomy version, which involves our opening question: Who gave the order? Moses says: "All of you came to me and said, 'Let us send men ahead of us to explore the land for us and bring back a report to us on the route we should follow and the cities we will come to.'" In others words, neither he nor God gave the order. The people initiated and demanded the sending of the spies!

But the author of Deuteronomy goes a step beyond, and along with the big rewrite come a few smaller renovations. In Numbers, the spies were the chieftains of their tribes: "From each of their ancestral tribes you shall send a man, every one a leader among them." In Deuteronomy, the spies aren't the chiefs, but simply representatives of the tribes: "I selected twelve of you, one from each tribe."

In Numbers, all the spies' names are listed; in Deuteronomy only Caleb son of Jephunneh and Joshua son of Nun are mentioned. In Numbers, the spies made their report to the entire nation; in Deuteronomy this matter is left unclear. In Numbers, the spies began by relating information and quickly moved to military assessments and political opinions about the odds of victory. In Deuteronomy, the spies were content with just the facts.

In Numbers, Caleb and Joshua told the people that the conquest would succeed with God's help: "Do not fear the people of the land, for they are our prey; their protection has departed from them, but the Lord is with us; do not fear them." Whereas in Deuteronomy, it was Moses who said: "Have no dread or fear of them. The Lord your God, who goes before you, is the one who will fight for you." Just as he did with *aleh resh*, Moses in Deuteronomy adopts Caleb's language from Numbers, along with his courage and faith.

Still, the more important difference has to do with that same age-old question that comes after any failure: Who gave the order? I stress again that in Numbers, the text says explicitly that this was God's initiative: "And the Lord spoke to Moses, saying: Send men, that they may spy the land of Canaan," and Moses did as he was told. But in Deuteronomy, Moses claims that the Israelites demanded the sending of spies and he agreed, and God is not mentioned at all.

The Moses of Deuteronomy, however, went beyond the "we are all guilty" pieties of today, by which the leadership and the people share the blame. According to him, the leadership is innocent and only the people are guilty. The people are guilty of sending the spies, of rejecting their findings, of faithlessness and defeatism. And because Deuteronomy is narrated in the first person, Moses got to rewrite his personal story as well, and took the opportunity to blame the people for the punishment he was given by God, who barred him from entering the land of Israel: "Because of you the Lord was incensed with me too, and He said: 'You shall not enter it either.' "

This is truly touching, but it contradicts what the text says it Numbers 20, where God commanded Moses to speak to the rock to draw water from it, but Moses struck it with his staff. God, true to form, was insulted; maybe the people would think that Moses drew the water and not he, and punished Moses and his brother Aaron: "Because you did not trust in Me, to show My holiness before the eyes of the Israelites, therefore you shall not bring this congregation into the land that I have given them."

In brief, we have before us a problematical author and editor, who have foolishly made God into a serial offense-taker, and *Moshe Rabbenu*—our Master Moses, in the traditional phrase—into a clumsy rewriter of history. Unfortunately, this is not the only such case in the Bible. The David of the book of Chronicles is not the same as the David of the book of Samuel. He too underwent some upgrading, whitewashing, and stain removal. But the author of Chronicles did not attribute the revisions to David himself, as did the author of Moses in Deuteronomy.

TWO SPIES, SECRETLY SENT

The Desert Generation passed away, and Moses with it. Joshua son of Nun, a principal player in the failed mission of the spies, became the leader of the entire people. Before crossing the Jordan and conquering the land, he too sent spies, the well-known pair who arrived at the home of Rahab in Jericho. Their story appears in Joshua 2, and the reader will discover that whereas the tale of the twelve spies is only of political interest, this one is also interesting on the level of operations. Moreover, it becomes clear that Joshua remembered well the espionage mission in which he had earlier taken part, and drew appropriate lessons.

First of all, he sent only two spies and not a dozen. Second, he sent professionals, "secretly sent two spies," secret agents expert in their field, not a bunch of tribal chieftains. His instructions prove the point: "Go, reconnoiter the region of Jericho." That was enough; they did not need ridiculously elementary explanations such as the twelve spies had received, to find out if the cities were fortified or open, and other obvious things. They were not asked to carry out superfluous missions such as the schlepping of grapes.

The way the two spies handled their operation shows professional familiarity with the task. When they got to Jericho they went at once to the home of the local prostitute, a character called Rahab. I am guessing that this name was not picked at random, but rather for its connection to the lady's profession, a link even clearer in English, since "Rahab" means "broad."

There were three reasons for choosing the home of a prostitute. First, there they would attract less attention. The local brothel is a natural venue for strangers, travelers from far away who seek such services. Secondly, in such a place there are all sorts of discussions to eavesdrop upon, or in which to take part and exchange news and opinions. Third, it is written of Rahab that "her house was upon the town wall, and she lived in the wall." This meant that one could escape straight from her window and be outside the city, even after its gates were closed. The reader is invited to recall another biblical visit to a prostitute in another enemy city, namely Samson's visit to the harlot of Gaza. Men of Gaza lay in ambush for him, and Samson was forced to rip out the gates of the city in order to escape. Joshua's spies were not endowed with Samson's muscles, but they were smarter than he was and knew what to expect. Rahab's house, sitting inside the wall, offered a means of escape.

Despite all the precautions, the king of Jericho got wind of the two strangers' visit. This suggests that the city had been put on high alert, owing to the proximity of the Israelites on the other side of the Jordan. The king demanded that Rahab hand the men over, but she hid them under stalks of flax that were drying on her roof, and told the king's soldiers that men had indeed been there, but had left.

Rahab was a smart woman. Total denial would have aroused suspicion, so she opted for a partial confession and even urged the king's men to pursue the spies. The soldiers rushed eastward toward the Jordan, while Rahab went up to the roof, to tell the two spies about the fear that had seized the people of Canaan at the news of the advancing Israelites. She cited the parting of the Red Sea and the victories the Israelites had won, and said: "All the inhabitants of the land melt in fear before you . . . As soon as we heard about it, we lost heart, and there was no courage left in any of us because of you."

In general, Rahab was remarkably knowledgeable about the Israelites and their God, far more so than might be expected from a simple Canaanite prostitute. The biblical author also made sure to give her a few amazing lines of dialogue. "I know that the Lord has given you the land," she said. "The Lord your God is indeed God in heaven above and on earth below." It is doubtful

that Rahab actually delivered such a political-theological manifesto on this occasion, but even if the reader disregards the
author's inflation of the facts, she was surely a wise and resourceful woman. She told the spies that their pursuers had gone
eastward and advised them to head for the hills: "Go towards
the hill country, so that the pursuers may not come upon you.
Hide yourselves there for three days, until the pursuers have returned; then afterwards you may go on your way."

Anyone familiar with the topography of the region knows
that "go towards the hill country" means "go west," the opposite
direction from the pursuers. In contrast with the flat plain east
of Jericho, this is a region of cliffs and twisting pathways where
the spies could easily hide, and also get a good view of the city
from on high.

In exchange for the information about Jericho, and for saving
the two spies, Rahab asked that her family and their property
be spared during the conquest of the city. The spies promised
her that the request would be met. She let them down through
the window by a rope and they did as she advised, hiding for
three days in the hills west of Jericho. Only after their pursuers
returned to the city did the spies slip eastward, to the Israelite
camp across the Jordan, whereupon the reader discovers that
Joshua had learned another important lesson from the episode
of the twelve spies: the secret agents did not get up in front of
the whole nation, as he and his eleven colleagues had done forty
years earlier. They reported only to him.

So much did the author wish to stress this point that he
wrote it three times in the same sentence: "They came to Joshua
son of Nun, and told him all that had happened to them, and
they said to Joshua." And what they said to Joshua was no less
than an exact quote of what Rahab had said: "For the Lord has

given all the land into our hands; moreover, all the inhabitants of the land melt in fear before us." This shows how trustworthy and important they considered her testimony to be.

Jericho was indeed conquered by means of a unique tactic, based on the information the spies obtained from Rahab. The priests of Israel, the *Cohanim*, carrying the Ark of God and blowing rams' horns, *shofarot*, walked around the city once a day for seven straight days, and the people marched with them in total silence. On the seventh day, they went around the city seven times, and the people, on command, gave a great shout, and the walls came tumbling down.

This event may be interpreted in two ways. The standard interpretation is that the fall of Jericho was one more miracle God performed for the Jews. But if this is so, the same question arises as when Moses sent the spies—why send them in the first place? It's enough to do God's bidding, and rely on miracles.

The other interpretation is that after the great shofar blasts of the seventh day, the Israelite soldiers stormed the city wall and destroyed it. This means that the seven days of marching around the city were intended to shatter the already shaky morale of the inhabitants of Jericho, and that Joshua indeed relied on Rahab's assessment thereof. Not by chance did he twice state that she should be looked after and saved. He said it once to the whole people, before the final blasts, and again to the two spies after the city had been conquered.

And indeed, in return for betraying her city, Rahab and her whole family were saved from death, "and she lives in Israel even to this day; because she hid the messengers, whom Joshua sent to spy out Jericho." It follows that quite possibly any number of Israeli citizens today, including some readers and perhaps also the writer of these lines, are descended from Rahab the harlot. I do not see this as a dishonor. On the contrary—this was an intelligent woman, whose beauty was praised by the rabbis of the Talmud in a manner that suggests she aroused not only their admiration, but their lust. They even added that she became a Jewess and married Joshua, and that the prophets Jeremiah, Ezekiel, and Huldah were her progeny.

THE ADVICE OF AHITHOPHEL

Spies were also active in the rebellion of Absalom. But these did not stop at intelligence gathering and were directly involved in events. In Second Samuel 15, we learn that Absalom's revolt was carefully planned over time. First, he tried to besmirch his father and ingratiate himself with the citizens of the realm. Then he sent spies—so it says in the text—throughout the tribes of Israel. Their job was not to collect information, but to wait for a signal from him and then announce, each of them, that Absalom had deposed his father and taken the throne.

The rebellious son also secretly recruited many supporters, including David's most senior and important counselor, Ahithophel the Gilonite, a singularly brilliant man whose advice was considered tantamount to the word of God. The organization and preparations went well, and when the rebellion began, David was in such bad shape that he was forced to flee Jersualem. He left ten concubines in the city to look after his palace, plus a few men: the priests Zadok and Abiathar, their sons Ahimaaz and Jonathan, and another chap named Hushai the Archite. Although the word "spy" is not attached to his name, Hushai was the most successful secret agent in all of the Bible. He ran a spy network more serious than any other in Scripture, penetrated the top leadership of the new regime, sabotaged plans, and dispatched information by means of couriers.

David was very disturbed that Ahithophel the Gilonite had joined up with his son. He instructed Hushai the Archite to pretend to be a supporter of Absalom and gave him two assignments. The first: "You will defeat for me the counsel of Ahithophel." And the second: "Whatever you hear from the king's house, tell it to the priests Zadok and Abiathar. Their two sons are with them there, Zadok's son Ahimaaz and Abiathar's son Jonathan; and through them you shall report to me everything you hear."

Since he was known as a friend of David's, Hushai came before Absalom with the hearty greeting "Long live the king!" Absalom was suspicious: "Is this your loyalty to your friend? Why did you not go with your friend?"

Hushai the Archite explained to Absalom that he preferred to follow the one who had been chosen by God and the people of Israel. He knew how important honor, appearances, and status were to Absalom. And Absalom indeed relished this toadying, and he let Hushai stay at his side.

Meanwhile, Ahithophel had begun to render his advice. First he advised that Absalom sleep with the concubines that David had left in the palace. That way, the people would know that the break between him and his father was final and irreversible, and they would support him. Absalom acted as Ahithophel said, and he did one better by sleeping with the concubines on the roof of the king's house, so everyone could see.

Then Ahithophel gave him more advice: to hurry and pursue David, before his father could get organized and assemble new forces. He suggested sending a special unit, with himself at the head, to capture David while he was "weary and disheartened" and kill only him, so that his loyalists would then follow Absalom.

Had Absalom followed this advice, the rebellion would have succeeded, with David dead and gone. But Absalom also wanted to hear the opinion of Hushai the Archite, who said: "This time the advice that Ahithophel has given is not good." He warned Absalom that his father and his mighty men were courageous fighters, enraged "like a bear robbed of her cubs in the field." He described David as a "valiant warrior, whose heart is like the heart of a lion," and he told Absalom that he faced defeat if he followed Ahithophel's plan. Instead he advised the full conscription of the nation's forces, with Absalom leading the troops into all-out war.

Hushai was not an accomplished strategist or tactician like Ahithophel, but he was psychologically insightful and well acquainted with the players involved. He knew that Absalom, a coddled prince with no battle experience, was terrified of his powerful father. He knew that Absalom, fond of pomp and glory, would prefer to appear at the head of a great army instead of sending out a force led by Ahithophel. Hushai thus gained vital time for David, since mustering a full army is not a matter of days, but takes weeks.

But what Hushai said next indicates something further: he knew Absalom was stupid. He therefore offered one more, especially foolish idea: if David holes up in a walled city, he said, we'll secure the city with ropes and pull it to the nearest ravine, where it will break into bits.

This is no ordinary dumb idea. This is one that the author of the Wise Men of Chelm stories would have paid good money to add to his compilation of nutty tales. By floating it, Hushai sought not only to thwart the advice of Ahithophel, but also to show Absalom's supporters what sort of idiot they had made their king. Amazingly enough, Absalom accepted Hushai's counsel over Ahithophel's, and so did all the Israelites. So peculiar was this choice that the biblical author felt compelled to explain that it was the Lord who turned things around, so that Absalom would be defeated by his father.

Hushai briefed the priests Zadok and Abiathar on what had transpired. They dispatched a maidservant to deliver the information to their sons Jonathan and Ahimaaz, who were waiting outside the city, and they passed it on to David along with a clear-cut recommendation: not to tarry on the road but to cross the Jordan that very night and organize his forces on the eastern bank.

Despite all the precautions taken by Hushai, the priests' sons were spotted as they made their way to David. Absalom sent soldiers to pursue them, but just as in the case of the spies sheltered by Rahab in Jericho, these agents of David found a woman to hide them from their pursuers and then send them safely on their way. David received the information and before the sun was up he had moved his whole army across the Jordan.

Ahithophel was a wise man. When his advice was rejected he realized Absalom would be defeated, that the rebellion would fail, and that he himself would suffer terrible punishment. He went home and hanged himself, thus assuring that he would not be tortured and die a villain's death, and his corpse be eaten by vultures. He was laid to rest in his ancestral plot, but he got his comeuppance another way. Somehow the phrase "the advice of Ahithophel" made its way into Hebrew usage as synonymous with bad, groundless, unjustified advice.

Thus was Ahithophel punished in a manner that not even he, for all his wisdom, could have foreseen. But history took its toll on Hushai too, and his name was forgotten—not just in our own time, but back in his day as well. In David's last testament

to his son Solomon he made mention of various characters who
were involved in the rebellion of Absalom. He commanded that
Joab, who slew Absalom, be killed, though not necessarily for
that act. The sons of Barzillai the Gileadite, who had provided
David with food when he camped across the Jordan, were to be
treated with favor. Shimei son of Gera, who had cursed David
as he fled from his son, was also to be killed. And Hushai the
Archite? The man who risked his life and saved David from his
rebellious son and his adviser Ahithophel? Surprisingly, Hushai
goes unmentioned in David's last will. But a man named Baanah
the son of Hushai was one of the twelve officials of Solomon
listed in First Kings 4. There is no way of knowing for sure, but
this may well have been the same Hushai the Archite, whose son
was repaid by David's son for services rendered by his father.

THE FIRST ANIMAL

The first animals mentioned in the Bible are the great *tani-nim*. They were created on the Fifth Day of Creation and are the only animals that the author of that story called by name. All the others are described more generally: "birds of the sky," "fish of the sea," and "beasts of the earth."

Although the great *taninim* have a name, no one knows what they were. Some say they were whales; some say they were mythological sea monsters whose creation by God was specifically cited to emphasize his superiority over them. The matter is not clear, so we will part from them with sad curiosity and move on to animals we know. Among these, the first to be mentioned in the Bible is the snake.

There are two creation narratives in the book of Genesis. In the first, we begin our relationship with animals on our left foot, in the other, on the right. In the first story, in chapter 1, the human being, male and female, is the last creature to be created, and is commanded to be fruitful and multiply and rule over the animals: "Be fertile and increase, fill the earth and master it; and rule the fish of the sea, the birds of the sky, and all the living things that creep on earth."

The second story, in Genesis 2, gets off to a better start. God created Adam alone and realized at once that this was a mistake: "It is not good for men to be alone," he said; "I will make a fitting helper for him." Contrary to conventional wisdom, the expression "fitting helper" did not refer to a human partner but to one of the animals or birds. Indeed, the God of Genesis 2 created the animals for this very purpose. He presented them to Adam so he might choose one of them to be his fitting helper. Adam named them all, but he was disappointed on the social level: "And Adam gave names to all the livestock and to the birds of the sky and to all the wild beasts; but for Adam no fitting helper was found." Whereupon the Lord cast upon him a deep sleep, took a rib from his body and from it fashioned a woman, which made Adam very happy.

It would seem that all had ended well, but then an unexpected problem arose. One of the animals created by God was the snake, and the snake tempted the woman to eat of the fruit of the Tree of Knowledge. The woman ate the forbidden fruit, gave of it to her husband as well, and the rest is well known: fig leaves, expulsion, a revolving sword, the pain of childbirth, earning bread by the sweat of your brow.

BETWEEN YOUR OFFSPRING AND HERS

Why did the snake pick the woman? Why did it tempt her and not the man? Why not both together? There are plenty of men in our world who would say that the snake knew very well what it was doing, that women are featherbrained and easy to tempt. Others will point out that the snake is a shopworn symbol of male sexuality, and its influence on the woman can also be interpreted in these terms.

In my humble opinion, the reason is otherwise. The snake seduced the woman because it wished to take her place. It wanted to be Adam's "fitting helper," and it had the right credentials: it was unusually intelligent, "the shrewdest of all the wild beasts that the Lord God had made," and was also endowed with speech, a human power that other animals lacked. These two qualities made it similar to Adam and worthy of his friendship. But Adam, as we have seen, preferred the woman. The snake, its expectations dashed, sought revenge, and perhaps it also wished to prove that Adam had made the wrong choice, and that it, not the woman, was fit to be the helper.

These motives become quite clear at the end of the story. God, it will be recalled, decreed specific punishments for each guilty party—man was sentenced to hard labor, woman to painful childbirth, and the snake would crawl on its belly and eat dirt. But for the snake he added an especially interesting sentence: "I will put enmity between you and the woman." In other words, not only regarding the temptation and eating the forbidden fruit, but also in the relationship between snake and mankind, the focus is on the woman. The hatred between the snake species and the human species would endure into future generations, "between your offspring and hers." Why "hers"? Because God knew that it was the woman whom the snake wished to injure, not Adam or the whole human race.

Beyond this particular case, it is worth noting that there is a similarity between the first two animals in the Bible, the sea monsters of the first creation story and the snake of the second narrative. Like the sea monsters, the snake is a frightening creature, dangerous, mysterious, with magical characteristics. Like the sea monsters, the snake represents, in extreme fashion, the human fear of all animals.

Indeed, despite the gentle breeze of friendship that floats through Genesis 2, where animals are created to be man's helpers, the animal world was not beloved of the authors of the Bible. This is made plain by God's very first commandment to man, which is to rule over the animals, to control and use them. This order was given even before man was created. The Lord said: "Let us make man in our image, after our likeness; they shall rule the fish of the sea, the birds of the sky, the livestock, the whole earth, and all the creeping things that creep on earth." In the opinion of the author of this creation story, domination over other living things is the purpose and mission of the human species.

A shame. It might have been hoped that the author would have given God, in his first words to mankind, something loftier and more ethical. There is no charity or faith in this opening line, no love, law, or justice, not even a religious commandment. Just divine permission to lord it over the animals. Is this the important thing, which needs to be said before anything else?

No doubt this message was written by an author with an agenda. It surely has to do with the fact that pagan religions had animals that symbolized deities and were considered holy. But it points to something else too: that despite the oppression, exploitation, and cruelty that characterize our relationship to animals to this day, and though we are smarter and stronger than they are, we are not comfortable with all that. We are so uncomfortable that we seek divine license and moral justification for our bad attitude. For this reason we invented the God-given permission to rule over them, from which would spring future zoos, slaughterhouses, hunting lodges, chicken coops, circuses, and dairies. The biblical dictum would also give rise to new breeds of pet dogs and tropical fish, and specialized milk cows, creatures that God neither made nor intended. Another result would be entire branches of human endeavor that would exploit animals: agriculture and cooking and fashion and warfare and entertainment and hobbies and sports. And also the notion that one nation had the right to rule and oppress and enslave another nation has derived from the most ancient of privileges we arrogated to ourselves in the name of God—the right to rule over the animals. Indeed, history teaches us time and again that all we need do is compare the other to an animal, reptile, monkey, dog, pig, or cockroach—and already we feel better.

PEOPLE TOGETHER WITH ANIMALS

The first person to make use of animals was Abel, the son of Adam and Eve. He was a shepherd, and sacrificed his first-born sheep to the Lord. God preferred Abel's lamb to the vegetarian offering of Cain, his brother the farmer. Meaning that when God gave us the right to eat animals, he was also thinking of himself.

A mere ten generations after Adam and Eve, Cain and Abel, the sea monsters, the sheep and the snake, the reader again encounters animals. Now he finds them in a uniquely interesting story, the tale of the flood, and in a place no less unique and interesting, Noah's Ark.

The background of the story is well known: The human race has abounded in evil and sin. The Lord regretted creating it, and decided to destroy it: "I will blot out from the earth the human beings I have created—people together with animals and creeping things and birds of the air, for I am sorry that I have made them."

But Noah, a righteous and blameless man, found favor in the eyes of the Lord. God instructed him to build a big ark out of wood, much bigger than was needed to save Noah and his family. The technical details of the ark, its materials and dimensions, may be studied by carpentry enthusiasts in Genesis 6. More important for our purposes is the divine order that Noah fill the ark with pairs of living creatures of every type, two by two, male and female, "of the birds according to their kinds, and of the animals according to their kinds, of every creeping thing of the ground according to its kind, two of every kind shall come in to you, to keep them alive." That is, the ark would contain couples that would serve as seeds of reproduction and ensure the perpetuation of the various species after the deluge.

The flood was God's sweeping response to the wicked behavior of mankind, and it is not clear to the reader why he decided to destroy the animals too. But one may be consoled that after giving man the right to rule and control animals, the Bible displays sensitivity to the preservation of animal life and an awareness of the ecological equality of man and animals.

Beyond that, Noah and God demonstrated greater enlightenment than one finds among the environmental organizations active today. Owing to subjective preferences, fund-raising concerns, and public relations, we care mainly about pandas and dolphins and somewhat less about rare spiders and endangered toads. It is easier and more pleasant to worry about irises and red peonies than about sundry nettles and brambles. But Noah, who could have taken advantage of the flood to get rid of mosquitoes and scorpions, for example, saved them. It may be safely assumed that even the oldest enemy of mankind, the snake, was not left out, and brought a mate along, so that after the flood the two could beget generations of snakes that would slither on their bellies and strike at our heels, and we would smack their heads. And I reckon that Noah also took aboard seeds, bulbs, and shoots. Nowhere is this written, but it makes sense, and it is well known that Noah planted a vineyard right after the flood, so he must have taken vine seedlings too.

In short, we have before us a heartwarming ecological tale. Everyone in the same boat: Noah, his wife, his sons and their wives, and pairs of mammals, insects, reptiles, and birds. But then comes one more detail, which people tend to forget. In Genesis 6, God told Noah to take one pair of each living creature, but in Genesis 7 he added: "Take with you seven pairs of all clean animals, the male and its mate; and a pair of the animals that are not clean, the male and its mate."

In other words, the principle of one pair of every species applies only to ritually unclean animals. Of the clean ones, seven pairs should be taken. One may wonder, by the way, how did Noah know which animals were clean and which not? After all, the dietary rules about cloven hooves and ruminant digestion had not yet been set down, nor had Jews or Judaism yet entered the world. But the story was intended for the reader and not for Noah, and by the time it was written and read, its readers knew something about the laws of kosher food.

A possible reason for the extra number of clean animals is that they would serve as food for the predatory creatures in the ark. But there is another interpretation, innocent if not disingenuous, which holds that God and Noah loved the clean animals in particular and wanted to save more of them. There were expert and experienced readers who believed this too. The rabbis of the Talmud wrote that toward the end of the flood, when Noah sent the raven to see if the waters were subsiding, the bird complained bitterly: "Your Master [God] hates me, and you hate me. Your Master hates me [since He commanded] seven [pairs to be taken] of the clean [creatures], but only two of the unclean. You hate me, since you leave the species of which there are seven, and send out one of which there are only two. Should the angel of heat or of cold smite me, would not the world be short of one kind?"

In the raven's opinion, God loves and favors the clean animals and hates the unclean ones, which is why he told Noah to take seven pairs of the clean ones, and only one pair of unclean creatures. But in the raven's view not only God, but also Noah, hates the unclean animals, and this is why he sent it, an unclean fowl of which there is but one pair in the ark, to check the water level. If something happens to me en route, grumbled the bird, if I freeze to death or am smitten by sunstroke, ravens would become extinct.

The raven is a smart bird and what he says makes sense, but soon enough the waters will recede, and the ark will open up, all its inhabitants will go out into the world, and the raven will be proven wrong. In the matter of the clean and unclean animals, God and Noah had different intentions entirely.

THE LORD SMELLED THE PLEASING ODOR

The passengers entered the ark in the six hundredth year of the life of Noah, on the seventeenth day of the second month, and left it on the twenty-seventh of the second month in his 601st year. In other words, for 375 days, a little over a year, Noah and his wife, and his sons and their wives, and all the animals lived inside the ark. Scripture tells us nothing about the quality of their shared life. One can imagine that there were tensions here and there, not to mention the stench, overcrowding, and tumult. But because conflicts and quarrels are absent from the text, it may be assumed as well that the passengers were able to maintain a passable, even positive, atmosphere.

The big surprise awaited them, the reader, and especially the clean animals, when the waters withdrew. The ark came to rest on the mountains of Ararat and the survivors of the flood came out of it. I like to imagine the animals jumping and running around, rolling and stretching, revitalized by physical exercise and happy to feel solid ground under their feet. And as for Noah, there is no need for guesswork, since the Bible tells us the first thing he did: "Noah built an altar to the Lord, and took of every clean animal and of every clean bird, and offered burnt offerings on the altar." In other words, he sacrificed them.

The deed is acceptable and even logical from a religious standpoint. Noah was grateful that he and his family had been saved, and in those days it was customary to thank God in proper fashion. The gods back then were not content with prayers, and the faithful expended much money on sacrifices. But from the point of view of the modern reader, especially one who till now may have seen the story of the ark as a manifesto of Greenpeace or the Sierra Club, there is a problem. The ark after all was a means of saving lives, and now Noah goes and slaughters living things, and not just any living things. Because the flood had destroyed all animals and livestock on the face of the earth, clearly the creatures sacrificed by Noah had been taken aboard the ark for this very purpose.

Only now does the reader understand the real reason for the divine command to take but a single pair, one male and one female, of each unclean species, but seven pairs of the clean ones. Not because of special fondness for them, or to feed them to panthers or lions, but so there would be creatures to sacrifice to the Lord at the end of the journey. It turns out that the raven, among the smartest of the birds, and the rabbis of the Talmud, among the smartest of men, were wrong. This is not a story of love and favoritism, but of ritual logistics. I hope that the raven, who had earlier claimed that God hated him, took a look at the kosher roebucks, pigeons, partridges, gazelles, and rams slaughtered on the altar, and understood that sometimes it pays to be unclean.

As for God himself, his reaction to the sacrifices, in particular to the aroma of their roasting flesh, is more problematic still: "When the Lord smelled the pleasing odor, the Lord said to Himself: 'I will never again curse the earth because of humankind, for the inclination of the human heart is evil from youth; nor will I ever again destroy every living creature as I have done.'"

The fact that God loves the smell of grilled meat, and that this smell inspires him to such important decisions of principle, is sad but not new. We have already seen it in the episode of Cain and Abel, and now again we see that so far as culinary tastes are concerned, he did not create us in his image but we created him in ours. But what is really shocking in the story is that even as God enjoyed the smell of the roasting flesh of living things, he promised not to harm them anymore. Was he concerned with their existence and their fate? According to this story, it would seem that God saved the living creatures from the waters so that he would not lack for sacrifices and burnt offerings after the deluge.

That is not all. After the flood, God gave Noah and his sons the same orders he gave Adam after the creation: "Be fruitful and multiply, and fill the earth. The fear and dread of you shall rest on every animal of the earth." In other words, a new era would not dawn for the unclean animals either. Noah did not take the animals into the ark to save them from the flood, but so that man would continue to have someone to rule over, exploit, and sacrifice to the Lord in the future. Nothing had changed. Even after the catastrophic flood, after the voyage together in the ark, God again defined the relationship of man and beast as one of fear, exploitation, and control.

A LION HAS ROARED, WHO WILL NOT FEAR?

L et us also look at the bright side. Despite the divine license to kill anything that moved, and despite the human talent for slaughter and extinction, back then we lacked the capacity we possess today for harming living things. We could not steal or poison their water supplies, destroy their natural habitat, or hunt them from off-road vehicles with high-powered rifles. The competition was more fair in those days.

Moreover, we must not ignore the fact that in antiquity animals represented a real threat to humans. Hosts of locusts, which even today can wreak enormous damage, could cause entire communities to die of famine. Wild animals stalked for prey alongside people's homes, attacking them and their flocks. There are any number of biblical tales about lethal encounters with lions and bears, and the words of the prophet Amos, "a lion has roared, who will not fear?" are not the product of the author's imagination but a reality of his time. In the book of Amos, another fine verse proves that such situations were common enough to serve as similes: "As if a man fled from a lion, and a bear met him, and went into the house, and leaned with his hand on the wall, and a snake bit him." And another example: "As the shepherd rescues out of the mouth of the lion two legs, or a piece of an ear; so shall the people of Israel who dwell in Samaria be rescued."

And yet, the Bible does not take a monolithic view of this subject. Alongside the tyrannical attitude to animals we also find an ecological approach that is truly progressive. The God of Genesis 1 created man last of all, within an orderly world that awaited his arrival, and gave him control over all living things. But the God of Psalm 104 ruled the world in an egalitarian fashion, and did not discriminate among wild animals, livestock, birds, and the human race.

The author of this Psalm loved the world of nature and knew it well. The reader will enjoy a discerning portrait of the interdependence of various living things and their environment:

> You make springs gush forth in the valleys;
> they flow between the hills,
> giving drink to all the wild animals;
> the wild asses quench their thirst.
> Beside them dwell the birds of the sky,
> they sing among the branches.
> From your lofty abode you water the mountains;
> the earth is satisfied with the fruit of your works.
> You make the grass grow for the cattle,
> and plants for people to use,
> to bring forth food from the earth . . .
>
> The trees of the Lord drink their fill,
> the cedars of Lebanon that he planted.
> Where the birds build their nests;
> The stork has her home in the junipers.
> The high mountains are for the wild goats;
> the rocks are a refuge for the badgers.
> He made the moon to mark the seasons;
> the sun knows its time for setting.
> You make darkness, and it is night,
> when all the animals of the forest stir.

The young lions roar for their prey,
seeking their food from God.
When the sun rises, they withdraw
and lie down in their dens.
Man then goes out to his work,
to his labor until the evening.
O Lord, how manifold are your works!
In wisdom you have made them all.

Human beings and animals are portrayed here as complete equals. God sustains them all with the same degree of attentiveness, and divides among them not only the bounty of the earth, but also the food-producing territories and the hours of activity.

In the book of Job, chapters 38 and 39, God also characterized himself as one who cares for all living things and knows their innermost secrets. He even peppered poor Job with a list of questions proving his point:

Can you hunt prey for the lion, and satisfy the appetite
of the king of beasts?

Who provides food for the raven, when its young ones cry
to God, and wander for lack of food?

Does the eagle soar at your command, and spread its
wings toward the south?

Do you know when the mountain goats give birth? Do
you mark the calving of the deer?

Who sets the wild donkey free? Who has loosed his
bonds?

Speaking to Job, God celebrates the passion for freedom of that wild donkey, who despite the dictum of Genesis 1 has not surrendered to the will of man: "I have given him the wilderness for his home, and the barren land for his dwelling. He scoffs at the tumult of the city, nor does he regard the shouts of the driver."

I am not sure that Job found solace for his afflictions in these descriptions of nature. He probably wished dearly to be like one of those living things that God cares about and does not torment the way God abused and tormented Job. But there is no doubt that these nature passages reflect informed interest in the subject, and a worldview different from that of the creation story.

A BIRD'S NEST

The biblical lawmaker, amidst his endless involvement with the minutiae of sacrifices and offerings, also addressed the welfare of various animals. In Deuteronomy 22, we find the fascinating and benevolent commandment known in Hebrew as *shiluah haken*, or "clearing the nest": "If you come on a bird's nest, in any tree or on the ground, with fledglings or eggs, with the mother sitting on the fledglings or on the eggs, you shall not take the mother with the young. Let the mother go, taking only the young for yourself, in order that you may fare well and have a long life."

Animal-rights advocates of today would protest this practice loudly. They would say that one should not take either the mother or the young from the nest. But this rule should be judged within its own context, wherein hunting and gathering were an essential means of human sustenance. True, in those days there were kings and noblemen who hunted for sport—the most disgraceful leisure activity known to man—but there were also common folk who depended for food not only on agriculture and the raising of livestock, but also on the hunting of wild animals. The *mitzvah* of "clearing the nest" was thus an ecological imperative, whose goal was to preserve the many species of birds.

The reasoning behind the commandment is clear: if one were to take the mother as well as the eggs and fledglings, an entire family would be destroyed, along with its future progeny. If only the mother were taken from the nest, the fledglings under her care would surely die. But taking the offspring, and letting her go, meant she could produce new ones and the species would be preserved.

It is interesting that in our own day the fulfillment of this enlightened *mitzvah* has become cruel and silly, and in direct opposition to its initial purpose. There was once a news item about an important rabbi from overseas who on a visit to Israel wished to add this *mitzvah* to the many already to his credit. A bird's nest was sought and found, and the righteous man went up a ladder, chased away the mother bird, and took the fledglings or eggs, as it is written in the Torah, but in complete violation of the spirit and context of the commandment's origin.

The biblical lawmaker also took notice of the hard lives of the domestic animals that served man in his fields and farms. He decreed, "You shall not muzzle an ox while it is threshing," that is, the mouth of the animal should not be muzzled, so it could nibble, now and then, the products of its threshing. The prohibition, "You shall not plow with an ox and an ass together" emanates from the likelihood that the pairing of two animals mismatched in size and strength would cause them both to suffer. The lawmaker ordered that we must even be kind to domestic animals belonging to our enemies: "When you see the donkey of one who hates you lying under its burden, and you would hold back from setting it free, you must help to set it free."

If we examine the words Abraham heard from his God during their various meetings, it would seem that apart from circumcision, the instructions and orders he was given applied to him alone: God commanded him to go to the land of Canaan, to change his name from Abram to Abraham and his wife's from Sarai to Sarah, to banish Ishmael to the wilderness, and to offer Isaac as a sacrifice. With all due respect, and due appreciation of Abraham's obedience, it is hard to call these things "commandments," "laws," and "teachings."

Neither did the generations preceding Abraham get from the Creator anything resembling a system of laws. The first instruction to be received by the human species was to be fruitful and multiply, and to dominate animals. This was a directive, and perhaps a sort of permission, but not a law. The second divine instruction, not to eat from the Tree of Knowledge, was likewise not a law in the conventional sense. It was given to Adam and is not binding or relevant for the rest of humanity, certainly not after the expulsion from Eden.

But in Genesis 9, right after the flood, there are listed a number of divine instructions known as the "Seven Commandments of the Sons of Noah." The word "law" does not appear there, though three verses, 4 to 6, do seem and sound like law, and are directed to all people, not just one person. There it is written: "But flesh with its life, which is its blood, you shall not eat," which means one may not eat the meat of a creature that is still alive. And more important still: "Whoever sheds man's blood, by man shall his blood be shed"—in other words, someone who kills another person will get the death penalty. The text does not specify if the murderer will be put to death by a righteous avenger or by a court of law, but the principle is most clear. One should not wait for punishment from the heavens: murderers will be killed in the framework of human society.

Is this what God meant when he spoke of the laws and commandments and teachings that Abraham heard and kept? Maybe, but I am dubious. The combination of "my command-ments," "my laws," and "my teachings" is too bold and formal to mean merely the few commandments of the Sons of Noah.

SIN IS LURKING AT THE DOOR

The two first sinners in the Bible are also its first two people. These were Adam, who at the time was still known simply as "the man," and Eve, referred to as "the woman." The two ate of the fruit of the Tree of Knowledge, not breaking any law but rather a specific injunction regarding that tree. Nor does their punishment speak of law and enforcement in the familiar form we find elsewhere in the Bible. Terrestrial courts of law did not yet exist, and even God did not act as lawgiver and judge. At first he warned them that if they ate of the Tree of Knowledge they would die, but later, when they disobeyed, he did not carry out his threat. He expelled them from the Garden of Eden and gave them another punishment entirely—hard labor and the pains of childbirth.

Despite the well-known expression "original sin" that de-rives from this event, the Hebrew word for sin, *het,* does not ap-pear here. It turns up for the first time only a generation later, when Cain and his brother Abel brought offerings to God. Abel, the shepherd, "brought of the firstlings of his flock and of the fat of it," and Cain brought "fruit of the ground." The Lord "had respect" for Abel's offering, "but for Cain and for his offering he did not have respect." Cain was filled with anger, and God, who could see what was coming, said to him: "If you do well, will you not be accepted? And if you do not do well, sin is lurking at the door; its desire is for you, but you must master it."

It's a fairly cryptic verse, but one may gather from it that the human heart is inclined toward evil. If man does good, and fights the evil imprinted within him, God will forgive him, "accept" him—and if not, he will have to deal with the sin on his own. Cain did not conquer his evil urge and killed his brother, but even he, the first murderer of the Bible, did not violate any law and was not punished by any court, for the only potential avengers, judges, and executioners were his parents, who were also the parents of the murder victim. The verb "to murder" also does not appear in the story, but rather the verb "to kill." Murder will be mentioned for the first time only in the Ten Commandments, and the prohibition against spilling blood comes a few chapters and generations after Cain, in the Commandments of the Sons of Noah.

God did not put Cain to death, but he punished him in a way that brings to mind the punishment his parents got for eating the forbidden fruit: the ground no longer yielded its bounty to him and he went to wander in the world. He built a city, "knew" his wife, sired sons. All of humankind was born of him and his brother Seth, who was born to Adam and Eve after the death of Abel. Thus it was Cain who propagated the human species, he and not Abel, God's favorite, who died without descendants.

Indeed, sin and crime remained part of the vocabulary and repertoire of human beings. In the days of Noah the earth became corrupt and filled with violence, and later on, the people of Sodom were "exceedingly wicked and sinners." In both cases, it is not clear which laws were broken by these sinners. But the stories suggest that mankind had already constructed a judicial system, as evidenced by Abraham's words to God: "Shall not the judge of all the earth deal justly?" Or as the men of Sodom taunted Lot: "This fellow came here as an alien, and he would play the judge!"

More examples follow. Abimelech the king of Gerar, who took Sarah after Abraham had presented her as his sister, complained to him, "In what have I offended you, that you have brought on me and on my kingdom a great sin?"—even though the Bible had yet to publicize the laws "Thou shalt not covet" and "Thou shalt not commit adultery." When Jacob groused that Laban had given him Leah for a wife, Laban said, "It must not be so done in our country, to give the younger before the first-born," which testifies to a system of law and custom that was in place in Haran. Later Laban accused Jacob of theft, as Joseph accused his brothers, even though the law "Thou shalt not steal" was not yet articulated in the Bible.

Jacob deceived his father, Rachel stole household gods from her father, Shechem son of Hamor raped Dinah, Reuben slept with his father's concubine, Potiphar's wife bore false witness against Joseph, and the fact that he was thrown into an Egyptian prison indicates a system of law and order. But the Bible speaks of all those sins and sinners without describing any legislation or "law"—apart from the vague "commandments," "laws," and "teachings" of which God spoke to Isaac.

THE FINGER OF GOD

It was more than four centuries later, following the Exodus from Egypt, that our laws were first proclaimed. In Exodus 18, Moses remarked to his father-in-law Jethro how hard it was to sit in judgment of the people: "When they have a matter, they come to me; and I judge between one and another, and I make them know the laws of God, and his teachings." But the "laws of

God" and "his teachings" were given only later, in chapter 20, in the collection known to this day by the marvelous name "The Ten Commandments."

Let me add parenthetically that the encounter on Mount Sinai, as later described in Exodus 31, produced another "first"— the very first written words of the Bible, inscribed upon the two tablets of stone. Until then nothing had been written, and nothing had been read. We spoke, told stories, wept, shouted, wished, and demanded—but did not write or read a single word.

The tablets of the law were not written by a human hand, but rather by "the finger of God." The first human writing is mentioned only much later in Deuteronomy, and the first reading comes with Joshua, who "read all the words of the Torah, the blessings and curses, according to all that is written in the Book of the Torah." This is also the first time that reading and writing are bound together, and it was long thereafter that the Jews were dubbed the People of the Book. What's most interesting, though, is that the first written material in the Hebrew Bible was not prose or poetry, but law.

The Ten Commandments are considered to this day to be the pinnacle, the basis, and the essence of Judaism. But reading them makes one wonder a thing or two: Why, for example, does it say "You shall not steal" but not "You shall not rape"? Why "Honor your father and mother" and not "Love your neighbor as yourself"? Why "You shall not bear false witness against your neighbor" and not "Honor the face of the old man"? And why ten commandments and not three, eight, twenty-six, or a dozen? Does the decimal system dictate the nature of the law?

The reader may also feel mild disappointment. Despite the long wait for the first Hebrew law, there is nothing new about a religious establishment that demands ritual exclusivity, and

nothing original in "You shall not kill" and "You shall not commit adultery," which are also written in the ancient legal codes
of non-Jewish nations. The prohibitions of theft and false witness are also common, and honoring one's parents is an important value in other cultures too. By the way, the reason given in
the Ten Commandments is even more of a letdown: "Honor your
father and your mother, that your days may be long upon the
land which the Lord your God gives you." In other words, not on
moral or spiritual grounds, or to strengthen family and community, but simply as a matter of personal interest.

We expected more, readers might well say, we expected
something truly special. Nevertheless, there is a certain uniqueness in the Ten Commandments. First of all, their existence as
a group and a foundation. Second, the way they were handed
down at Mount Sinai before an entire people who witnessed
signs and wonders. Third, the Ten Commandments do include
three great innovations: monotheism, the Sabbath, and "You
shall not covet."

YOU SHALL HAVE NO OTHER GODS BESIDE ME

For some reason, monotheism is considered a superior and
progressive innovation, while polytheism is thought of as
an inferior and primitive concept. I understand why it is preferable to believe in an abstract God, thus removing the divine
status of the powers of nature and the stars and the Zodiac, not
to mention idols made of wood and stone. But I don't understand
why one god is preferable to several.

Sometimes I amuse myself with the possibility that Moses
invented or embraced monotheism for a simple, almost technical
reason: it's a lot easier to tramp through the desert with one ark
of one God, than to carry around in that blazing heat a whole

passel of gods, supplying each one with a tent, cold drinks, and sacrifices. But the truth is that the Bible does not present a consistent and comprehensive notion of monotheism. Throughout Abraham's entire discourse with God, the singularity of God is never mentioned. Neither did Isaac or Jacob deal with the idea of monotheism, except for the Lord being their God and the God of the nation that would spring from their loins.

Even at the burning bush, in his first revelation to Moses, God did not speak about his uniqueness but instead said he was the God of Abraham, Isaac, and Jacob. And when Moses stood before Pharaoh and spoke to him in the name of God, he called him "the God of Israel," a statement that leaves room for the possible existence of other gods of other nations.

Indeed the Bible is filled to overflowing with hints and evidence of the existence of other gods. Even in the Song of the Sea, after the parting of the Red Sea, there appears a line that is manifestly non-monotheistic: "Who is like you, O Lord, among the gods?" As if to say, there are plenty of gods, but not one of them matches up to the God of Israel.

And not only in the Torah, the Pentateuch, do we find such a thing. When Elijah competed with the prophets of Baal in a rain-making contest, he suggested to them: "You call on the name of your god and I will call on the name of the Lord." And the prophet Micah said: "For all the peoples walk each in the name of its god, but we will walk in the name of the Lord our God forever and ever." These verses also point to other gods alongside our own.

The Hebrew language itself suffers from a lack of clarity regarding the oneness of the Almighty. The word *Elohim*, one of the synonyms for "God," is in plural form, although the verbs attached to it are generally in the singular. In the very first verse of the Bible it says, "In the beginning *Elohim* created," using *bara* for "created" and not *bar'u*, the plural form. Yet later in the same chapter, God talks about himself in the plural: "Let us make man in our image, after our likeness," and afterward he goes back to the singular. Perhaps this was the first use of the "royal we." But the medium of Endor, who raised Samuel's spirit from the dead, said to King Saul: "I see *Elohim* coming up from the earth," where "coming up" appears in plural form. And in Joshua 24:19, Joshua son of Nun says that God is "a jealous God" in the singular and "*Elohim kedoshim*" in the plural: "holy gods." Similarly, today's spoken Hebrew uses the figurative expression "*Elohim gadol*"—meaning "anything can happen"—where God is plural and *gadol* ("great") is singular, but also "*Elohim adirim*" with a plural adjective, which means "good God!" or "holy cow!" This latter idiom, by the way, derives from a Philistine cry in First Samuel 4: "Who will save us from the power of this mighty God?"—*Elohim adirim*.

Even the first commandment is not free of this linguistic ambiguity. It is written: "I am the Lord your God . . . You shall have no other gods beside me." Any teacher of grammar, seeking to inculcate the agreement of subject and object, would have a hard time explaining why the Hebrew for "other gods" is plural, *Elohim aherim*, whereas the construction "you shall not have" involves the future singular of the verb "to be," *yihiyeh*, and not the plural *yihiyu*. It could be that behind all this is the fine and interesting notion that just as God has no material body, neither does he have a grammatical one.

But if we drop the Hebrew linguistics and focus on the content, we find that the first commandment is saying something else entirely. It allows that other gods may exist, but says it is forbidden to worship them. In other words, it is not the singularity of God that is established in the Ten Commandments, but that he is the one and only God of the Children of Israel.

Now consider the most important, moving, and fundamental verse in all of Judaism: "Hear, O Israel; The Lord our God is one Lord." This, the famous *Shema Yisrael*, would seem to be the highest expression of the principle of monotheism, yet it is not necessarily so. Here too the words "the Lord our God" suggest the possible existence of gods that are not "ours," but those of others. And "one" may be understood as our one God, but not the only one in the world.

On the subject of the singularity of God, the clearest statement in the Bible appears in Isaiah 44: "I am the first, and I am the last; and beside me there is no God." God is described here as the only God, everywhere and at all times—and this, by the way, is the source of Jesus's words in the book of Revelation: "I am the Alpha and the Omega, the first and the last." But earlier than either of these verses is the statement from Deuteronomy 4:36: "There is no other beside him."

The full verse spoken by Moses to the Israelites is this: "To you it was shown, that you might know that the Lord is the God; there is no other beside him." Apart from the clear syntax, in which "the Lord"—in the Hebrew, the sacred tetragrammaton YHWH—is God's name, and "the God," *ha-Elohim*, serves as a definition, the text provides a brief, unambiguous slogan, the envy of any copywriter.

Thus it comes as no surprise that it is the catchy phrase "there is no other beside him"—five simple syllables in Hebrew, *ein od milvado*—and not the marvelous, enigmatic *Shema*, that one finds pasted today on the rear windows of Israeli cars.

That one, and the popular bumper sticker "God, We Love You," proclaim that the Almighty guides the wheel of the car in front of you. All this is of a piece with the dumbing down of today's Israeli Judaism, where lucky charms, pop Kabbalah, born-again Orthodoxy, religious political parties, and the graves of holy men hold sway.

GOD IS ONE

Modern man, as we have noted, tends to regard monotheism as a lofty spiritual ideal, yet it might be interesting to examine it from the standpoint of God as well. From his point of view, it would seem, this is a serious problem, maybe the cruelest blow dealt him by his believers. Worse than straying after other gods or violating the Sabbath or eating crabs on the Fast of Gedaliah is making the Lord our God one God.

It is not good to be a God alone. Whereas the gods of Greece, Rome, Egypt, and Babylon had a rich and stimulating social life, begat children, quarreled and took revenge, fell in love and cheated on each other, made war and had fun, the Lord our God lives alone. And so, beyond our mutual complaints, his and ours, which often resemble the spats of a long-married couple, lurks a deep and ancient rupture: God banished us from the Garden of Eden and sentenced us to lives of toil and pain, and we invented monotheism and sentenced him to a life of barren loneliness.

In the book of Genesis there are hints of better times in the social life of God. As I noted earlier, his first words about himself, in Genesis 1, are spoken in the plural: "Let us make man in our image, after our likeness," which could have been said to a whole group of gods. Indeed, at the beginning of Genesis 6 we are told of intriguing characters known as "the sons of Elohim." Did God have children and a wife? Or maybe two? Sixteen?

Seventy? And the sons of Elohim—were they also gods? The Bible offers us no answer, but the rest of the story attests to a very good relationship between the sons of Elohim and the human race: "The sons of Elohim saw how beautiful the daughters of men were and took wives from among those that pleased them." The daughters of men bore children of the sons of Elohim, and these were "the heroes of old, the men of renown."

This story, a vestige of an ancient and mysterious layer of Israelite religion, points to a playful polytheistic phase that was surely to God's liking. And it's not the only such story. In the first chapter of the book of Job, it is written: "Now there was a day when the sons of Elohim came to present themselves before the Lord, and Satan came also among them." Here too we find a lively family group, with God receiving guests, making bets, hearing and telling stories. He may also be serving refreshments, and there is no doubt he is having a good time.

But in the greater bulk of the Bible God exists and acts alone, with decidedly gloomy consequences. Because miracles and wonders start to get boring, even to him, and handling the weather takes up little of his time, earthquakes have become redundant and the supervision of evolution and various biotopes has hardly changed in millions of years—beside which he has no other gods or goddesses to pass the time with, in conversation or a meal, or love or a good fight—God is busy with his believers, to whom he devotes far too much time and attention.

And indeed, whoever reads the Bible of the solitary God discovers that now and then he is portrayed in embarrassing ways. The creator of heaven and earth, splitter of the Red Sea, Lord of Hosts, is depicted by various authors as petty and annoying, jealous, insulted, complaining. He threatens, he promises, he regrets. He wants praise and craves glory. He makes accusations, he stalks and catches red-handed, he keeps score of the gifts he gave us and threatens to return the ones we gave him. On the verge of tears in the book of Jeremiah, he remembers the good days of young marriage, when we followed him into the desert, an unsown wildnerness.

Gods like Baal and Zeus did not come to their believers with such complaints. Their authors made sure to supply them with their consorts Astarte and Hera, and bands of nymphs and concubines, and children legitimate and otherwise, relatives, friends, rivals, neighbors, and colleagues. But the Lord our God is One, we have no other beside him and he has no others except us. This seems the true reason for the invention of monotheism. We created a lonely God so he would attend to us alone.

YOU SHALL NOT DO ANY WORK

The second innovation of the Ten Commandments is the Sabbath. It appears, and is sanctified, back at the beginning of the second chapter of the Bible, as the blessed day on which God rested after the six days of Creation. But in the Ten Commandments there is the added prohibition: "You shall not do any work, you, nor your son, nor your daughter, your manservant, nor your maidservant, nor your cattle, nor your stranger that is within your gates." Why, by the way, is "your wife" not included among those deserving of rest? That's how it goes in the Bible: somebody has to serve food to the men and clear the dishes from the table, even on Shabbat.

Many words have been penned about the Sabbath by fine writers more devout than I, so I shall make do with a few comments. First of all, even those, like me, who drive their cars on Shabbat, listen to music, and switch on the electric teapot, also rest from their labors on this day and thank Moses and God for this fabulous idea, which other cultures and religions have copied with enthusiasm. Indeed, the Sabbath is a social and psychological concept that was surprisingly progressive for its day. It was established at a time when kings ruled their subjects absolutely. Polygamy, and the abuse and honor killing of women, were routine. Slavery was widespread, compulsory education was not yet mandated, children were enslaved and sacrificed, adulterers were stoned to death, and a tooth was exacted for a tooth and an eye for an eye. And all of a sudden, this enlightened, liberal, egalitarian, and futuristic notion—the Sabbath.

Beyond its social value, the seventh day of rest is also the reflection of an interesting biblical worldview, namely, that work is not a privilege, mission, or ideal, but a burden and even a punishment. This is how it is presented in its earliest appearance, as the punishment imposed upon us for man's original sin: "By the sweat of your brow shall you eat bread."

But for all my fondness for Shabbat and my appreciation for whoever dreamed it up, the most interesting and provocative of the Ten Commandments is the tenth: "You shall not covet." I would assume that sooner or later, other lawgivers in other cultures would have come around to the Sabbath, but "You shall not covet" is the most unusual and original commandment of them all, unparalleled to this day.

YOU SHALL NOT CRAVE

Many have pondered the meaning of the final commandment. Does "You shall not covet" prohibit the thought, the sheer craving itself, or must the thought be accompanied by action? This is not a simple matter. Coveting can be the reason for an illegal act, such as murder, rape, or robbery, but it can also be the reason for a positive and desirable act, such as work or purchase. Besides, if "You shall not covet" speaks of active implementation, there would have been no need for "You shall not commit adultery" or "You shall not steal," for example, since these are actions taken by the coveter to achieve his wish.

I shall not survey the range of opinions already voiced on this question. But it is worth keeping in mind that the Ten Commandments appear not only in Exodus 20, but also in Deuteronomy 5. In the Exodus version, the tenth commandment goes like this: "You shall not covet your neighbor's house, you shall not covet your neighbor's wife, or his male or female slave, or his ox, or his ass, or anything that is your neighbor's." Whereas in Deuteronomy, it reads: "Nor shall you covet your neighbor's wife, nor shall you crave your neighbor's house, his field, or his male or female slave, or his ox, or his ass, or anything that is your neighbor's."

It is easy to notice the small change in the objects of the coveting and the order of their appearance, but the important thing is that in Deuteronomy we also find the synonym "crave." This means that the authors of Deuteronomy felt a need to clarify this problematic point, and determined that "You shall not covet" applied to craving itself, just the thought, even without action attached.

This interpretation is supported by other biblical verses. The book of Proverbs warns against a temptress: "Covet not her beauty in your heart." In other words, coveting is the internal desire, not the action. And in the book of Micah it is written: "And they covet fields, and take them by violence." Here too a clear distinction between the covetous thought and its realization through violence. In the preceding verse, the prophet Micah describes such criminals as "those who devise iniquity, and work evil," which also differentiates between thought and deed.

For the sins of theft and murder, disrespect of parents, adultery, Sabbath violation, taking God's name in vain, and bearing false witness, the Torah prescribes clear-cut punishments, as a matter of law. But nowhere is it specified how a coveter is to be punished. There is thus a sharp legal distinction between a violator of the first nine commandments, whose sins may be proven and witnessed, and the transgressor of the tenth. In the terrible case of David and Bathsheba, the prophet Nathan did not cry out when the king saw Uriah's wife bathing and lusted after her, but only after the crimes to which the coveting led—committing adultery with her, and murdering her husband. Nor did the prophet Elijah confront King Ahab when the latter coveted the vineyard of Naboth and tried to buy it—a lawful move, to be sure—but stepped in only after Jezebel had arranged for the trumped-up trial of Naboth, the false witness borne against him, and his death by stoning, and the expropriation of his vineyard.

And so, a moment before completing the list, after nine clear commandments of "do" and "don't do," Moses and the Lord came up with their surprising "You shall not covet," which is neither. It does not command or forbid any doing. It means: you must not crave, lust, or desire. And also: you shall not think forbidden thoughts. And even: do not dream, do not imagine.

It's strange. In general, the authorities are only interested in prohibited actions, statements, or plans. Even dictators and inquisitors are not able to supervise what is in one's heart. Not that they're not interested, but they know they cannot jail the spirit, to chain the passion and envy, the hope and the dream.

Can it be that "You shall not covet" is the zenith of totalitarianism, an example of a theocracy so dark that it seeks to oversee thought as well? I don't think so. Such an outlook requires not only wickedness but stupidity, and it's hard to impute those qualities to the biblical lawgiver.

Yet why were the Ten Commandments sealed with such a strange demand? With a law that cannot possibly be fulfilled or enforced? I take the liberty of assuming that it was not a case of error or wickedness or foolishness or just a whim. If Moses topped off the Ten Commandments with one that nobody can keep, it's a sign that this is exactly what he had in mind.

YOU DO NOT KNOW WHICH SHALL SUCCEED

The ambiguity of the last commandment is rooted in the traditional division of the whole set. It is customary to say that the first commandments deal with matters between man and God, and the later ones have to do with interpersonal relations. In my opinion, however, "You shall not covet" is not about other people, but concerns sins that a person keeps to himself. That, and its position in the list, is where its meaning lies.

Moses did not just happen to put "You shall not covet" in last place among the Ten Commandments. Up till that point, the commandments all seem demanding and obligatory, yet easy enough to fulfill: most readers honor their parents, do not murder, do not worship other gods or bow down to idols or pictures. Here and there may also be found citizens who never steal, do not bear false witness, always observe the Sabbath, and do not commit adultery. Thus the reader may check off the first commandments with satisfaction, some taking credit for five and others eight or nine, and feel they are doing what is right in the eyes of the Lord, more or less—but then comes that last commandment, and the reader understands that he will never fully satisfy the will of the Creator.

Everybody covets. One time or many, once a year or twice

a day. In a troubling and painful way, or playfully, just kidding. In a depressing and paralyzing manner, or in a manner that is useful and productive. Coveting the neighbor's house, his ox, his talent, his wife, her husband. Craving his car, his donkey, his looks and status. Dreaming of the greener grass of his home, his bed, his brain, his wallet and his job. I would assume that even righteous *tzadikkim*, great Torah scholars, even rabbis and religious judges whose righteousness extends to the highest and holiest reaches of Israeli politics, are not perfect in this regard, are not innocent of one sort of coveting or another.

Everyone fails the last commandment, which is how organized religion created its ideal condition: man's perpetual feeling of guilt toward his God, and the knowledge that he cannot fulfill God's will. In this way, the Ten Commandments created the perpetual need of the believer for the mediation of the religious establishment, in exchange for the fees and tithes first described in the book of Exodus.

"You do not know which shall succeed, either this or that, or whether they both alike shall be good," says Ecclesiastes, expressing the dilemma of man, who stands before his God hoping to satisfy his will. As opposed to Ecclesiastes, the Ten Commandments tell the reader what will succeed and what won't, but the last one prevents total success. Thus, the biblical lawgiver made sure that no Jew would ever get a perfect ten in the test of the commandments. Nine is the highest score on the Jewish report card.